How to Become A Candidate Master

Alex Dunne

Thinkers' Press 1985

2nd Edition: September 1986

ISBN: 0-938650-39-4

Request for permissions and republication rights should be addressed in writing to Thinkers' Press,
1026 Arlington Court
Davenport, Iowa 52803.

How to Become A Candidate Master

To Yolanda

CONTENTS

INTRODUCTION
For Category I Players

It is a common dream of chess players to visualize themselves as master players, defeating their opponents, winning tournaments. Such are the stuff of dreams but, before we can run, we must first learn how to walk. As a Category I (Class A) player you have already lifted yourself above the majority of tournament players. As a matter of statistics, with a rating of 1800+, 83% of all tournament players are ranked below you.

Above you, however, are some pretty strong players–the World Champion, the Grandmasters, the Masters, and, our target, the Candidate Masters (experts). Roughly speaking, the World Champion is defined as the player who consistently (3 out of 5 or better) defeats all the Grandmasters he faces. A Grandmaster, roughly defined again, defeats Masters in 3 out of 5 games or better. The Master will consistently defeat the Candidate Master by the same ratio or better, and the Candidate Master has been defeating you by that same edge. Why?

The simplistic answer is that the Candidate Master plays better chess than the Category I player. It is the design of this book to reveal the differences in play to the category I player to enable him to become a Candidate Master.

The typical chessbook uses a different approach. Most books select Master games analyzed by Masters in an attempt to raise a player immediately to the Master level. Though these books are extremely valuable and sometimes very well written, the fact is that, there is simply no easy road to masterhood. As a Category I player, you are quite aware of the struggle, work, study, and pain it took to get you this far. Of course, there are rewards and joys in playing as well as you do too. It is not easy to become a Candidate Master but with the aid of this book, some perseverance, work and study, some joy in your chess, that goal can be obtained.

This book, then, differs from others in that the games contained within are games between Category I players and

How to Become A Candidate Master

Candidate Masters. These games were selected from recent (1982) U.S. tournaments. In these games we will see the typical strengths and weaknesses of the Category I player and we'll discuss how the expert, usually, takes advantage of them.

When you play over these games you will take the side of the Candidate Master. If you are going to learn to play like a Candidate Master you may as well sit in his chair. A word of warning–you will not win every game from the Candidate Master's (CM) seat. No Candidate Master can so dominate Category I players, just as no Category I player can expect 100% results against Category II players; there are lessons to be learned from losses and draws as well as wins.

I have one final word about studying these games–there are fifty chapters in this book, fifty tournament games. These games were played with a clock running, ticking away. It is one thing to study games in the quiet of your den, it is another thing, again, to play a tournament game. Since your intention, presumably, is to become a Candidate Master in the tournament arena, not an armchair expert, the best way to study this book is one (or possibly two) games a day, with a chess clock running by your side. Take a 3x5 index card to cover up the moves. A small rectangle can be cut out of the left hand side to reveal White's move and still cover up Black's response when you are "playing" the black pieces. If you want to record your choices, you may. This would give you a guide to compare your choice of moves against the Candidate Master's choice.

Alex Dunne
Sayre, PA

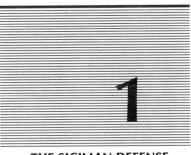

THE SICILIAN DEFENSE

One question that as a Category player you have already solved is "what opening should I play?" You have more than likely discovered what openings suit your style and personality. It has been said that most tournament players play the openings like Grandmasters, the middle game like experts, and the endings like children. This holds true, to a large extent, at any level below Master. Memory, study, a familiarity with opening principles means that most games are decided in the middle game or later with only a small percentage of games actually being decided in the opening.

If you desire a closer study of the openings, one of the best ways to gain a deeper understanding is to purchase one of the better opening manuals, and then study your tournament games with regard to the openings, or play correspondence chess with the intent of gaining depth in your opening study, or both.

1. e4 c5 2. Nf3 d6 3. d4 cxd 4. Nxd4 Nf6 5. Nc3 a6

To play 6. Bg5 in tournament play, the White player must be very well booked on the Poisoned Pawn line 6... Qb6. This well-analysed line is critical in the selection of a line to choose in playing against the Najdorf Sicilian. As a Category I player you may choose a less-analysed line. In this game, the Sozin will be played. Is this a good choice? In the struggle to win, it is as good as any variation.

6. Bc4 Qc7

A small success has happened here that you, as a Candidate Master (you had better get used to the title–we will be calling you that throughout the rest of the book. All that you need do is go out and earn the title) are aware of: Black has left "book" by this not unusual move. This leaving may be harmless or important. The job of the Candidate Master is to determine how important the variation is. So, how important is this digression? Analyse.

How important is an opening "Innovation"? the Candidate Master would do well to learn from the philosophy of Grand Master Bogoljubov: "When I have the white pieces, I have the advantage because I am white. When I have the Black pieces, I have the advantage because I am Bogoljubov." All opening innovations by Category I players should be looked upon as errors until the Candidate Master cannot prove otherwise.

7. Bb3 e6 8. f4 Nc6 9. 0-0

What is wrong with this move? Players who know the Sozin will be familiar with the trap: 9... Nxd4 10. Qxd4 d5 11. Kh1 Bc5 12 Qd3 dxe 13. Nxe4 Nxe4 14. Qxe4 0-0 with a good game for Black. When you play a Sozin, you should be familiar with the freeing strategy which can appear in different forms.

A valuable lesson appears next: both sides are unfamiliar with this trap. This is indicative of poor opening preparation. The importance of this lesson? It is all right–within reason–to err the first time you play a particular opening. By the next time you try it, you should have learned from your own games by reviewing and studying them after the tournament.

9... b5 10. Be3 Bb7

Another recurring theme in the Sozin is the gambitting of the e-Pawn by 10... b4 11. Na4 Nxe4 12 f5 with lots of central play for White. This idea, too, appears in many forms in the Sozin. Is it sound? The Candidate Master should explore the lines himself, deciding which side he would rather play. Five-minute chess and correspondence chess with this line can be beneficial. In OTB play with the clock ticking against a Category I player, the chances are all with White.

11. f5

Thematic play–White is trying to weaken the Black central formation. The e-Pawn is still very delicate. Can Black take it by 11... Nxd4 12. Bxd4 e5 13. Be3 Nxe4? You should visualize this combination of moves. After 14. Nd5, Black has too many difficulties. If you can visualize this, you are already well on your way to being a Candidate Master.

11... e5 12. Nxc6 Qxc6

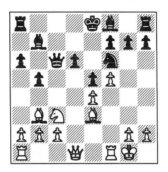

In this diagram you need a plan. What is White's target? If you have pinpointed the King stuck in the center, you have the killer instinct necessary for promotion. If you selected to defend the e-Pawn, you are violating a basic truth in chess. White has made logical, mostly sound, opening moves. He leads in development: there should be no reason for White to have to defend at this stage. This lesson is a hard one to learn and we will see it again and again in the conflict of Category I vs. Candidate Master.

13. a4 b4 14. a5

King in the center!

14... 0-0-0 15. Bd5 Nxd5 16. Nxd5 Kb8

By now your adrenalin should be moving. The Black King is no better here than it was on e8. Attack is the order of the day. If Black is allowed to survive, his two Bishops will give him some chances. In the boxing ring, a reeling opponent must be knocked out before he gets a second wind and starts hitting you back.

17. Qd2 Qc4

Better defense, but probably inadequate in the long run was 17... Qb5. What do you do against this move? If you saw 18. Qxb4 Qxb4 19. Nxb4 Bxe4 20. Nxa6+ you are too interested in Pawns. That was a King you were hunting one move ago. Now you settle for a Pawn? For shame. Check out 18. c4!

But more to the point: 17... Qc4?! is an error. Why? It is true a Grandmaster can defend difficult positions tenaciously, but your opponent is not a GM. Defense is much more difficult than attack; in bad positions, blunders are easy to find.

18. Ra4 Qc6 19. Rxb4 Rc8 20. Qf2

Also good was 20. Rb6.

20... Re8 21. Ba7+ Ka8

Work out the attack after 21... Ka8 (There are many wins. Simple is 22. b3)

22. Rc4 Black Resigns

That was a demolition job–and good chess. Good chess is the goal of the Candidate Master. If you can do it once, you can do it again.

1. c4

Opening preference is quite prone to fads. In the 1980's the English Opening is one of the most popular first moves, mainly because it is less analysed. As a Candidate Master you need to be prepared to fight the English. There are several good plans, some of which you shall see later. This game we are going to see a gambit line designed to seize the initiative.

This gambit continues 1... Nf6 2. Nc3 e6 3. e4 d5 4. e5 Ne4 5. Nxe4 dxe4 6. Qg4. To choose this gambit, you must be willing to gamble that White will not defend well. This is not a bad gamble if you have an aggressive chess temperament.

1... Nf6 2. Nc3 e6 3. e4

One of the reasons the English is popular is its flexibility. White may play 3. d4 when the opening can transpose into a Queen's Gambit (... d5) or a Nimzoindian (... Bb4) or Benoni (... c5). White sidesteps all of these, intending to play "positional chess" like "the Grandmasters do." Such an attitude on White's part makes the gambit line all the more attractive.

3... d5 4. e5 Ne4 5. Nxe4 dxe4 6. Qg4

Well, gambiteer, how to continue? You should see that 6... Qd4 is easily met by 7. Nf3, so the e-Pawn is dead. You should check an opening book for 6... Nc6. Black elects a different idea.

6... Bd7 7. Qxe4 Bc6 8. Qe3?!

Gambit positions like this are difficult for Class A players to defend. We will not discuss the merits of 8. Qf4 over 8. Qe3. You are playing the Black forces. White has an extra Pawn, but is slightly disorganized. Your plan?

8... Na6

Taking advantage of the Queen on e3. The threat is ... Bc5 gaining more time and ... Nb4 with brutal threats.

9. d4?!

White misses the best defensive try by 9. a3. Even after the best defense, Black's gambit has succeeded in making White's game very difficult. Why is this? It is because Category I players are much better attackers than defenders. Whether it is worth a Pawn to put the Category I player on the defensive is a question you must not only ask yourself, but answer, too.

9... Nb4

This formation, too, is one an expert must be familiar with. Aside from the obvious threat of ... Nc2+ Black has the secondary threat of ... Qxd4; Qxd4 Nxc2+ winning back the Pawn with an excellent game.

10. Kd1

How does Black take advantage of White's King in the center? The immediate try 10... Bc5; 11. Ne2 doesn't seem to lead to anything. Plan?-Think this over. How about a Rook on d8?

10... Qh4!? 11. Nf3?!

After 11. a3, Na6 12 Bd2 White has chances to survive.

11... Bxf3+! 12. gxf3 Rd8

Diagram

The gambit has worked. If White had been a Master, it more than likely would have failed, but 1801 is a long, long way from 2200+. Practical chess? Your decision.

13. f4 Bc5 14. Ke2 Nc2

Note that an expert still thinks *King*. The Knight reattacks d4.

15. Qe4 Nxd4+ 16. Ke1 Bb4+ 17. Bd2 Bxd2+ 18. Kxd2 Nb3+ 19. Kc3 Nxa1 20. Be2 Qxf2 21. Rxa1 c5!

Black could also have castled, but this move announces Black's intention to continue the attack. The threat of Qd4+ simplifying into a winning endgame forces White into further simplification.

22. Rd1 Rxd1 23. Bxd1 0-0 24. Bc2 g6

Overlooked the mate? Not a Candidate Master player! There is no hurry to play ... Qd4+. The coming invasion of the d-file will end the contest. How does the Candidate Master know this? One way is through experience. Another is faith – the Rook should beat the Bishop in this position...this is faith in the truth of chess. The last is calculation: if White plays Qxb7, Qxf4 will free Black's Kingside Pawns to make a new Queen.

25. Kb3 Qxh2

Candidate Masters do not play like Masters (That's another book). Better was 25... Rd8 but the expert knows how to win this position. His plan, an undefeatable one, is ... Qxh2, Q away, h5, h4, h3, h2, h1(Q) and mate. The Candidate Master should always plan how to win from a winning position. Any winning plan will do.

26. Qxb7 Qxf4 27. Qc7 Qe3+!

Be alert! Though ... h5-h4 would win easily, the Candidate Master always keeps an eye on the King. The great Siegbert Tarrasch, world championship contender, expressed it thus, "When you see a good move (... h5) sit on your hands and see if you can find a stronger one."

28. Ka4 Qd2 White Resigns

1. e4 e5 2. Nf3 Nc6 3. Nc3

The Four Knights Game was very common eighty years ago but became over-analysed and faded out of popularity, with the reputation of being too drawish. Still the opening has its advantages: it is very safe for White, there are many traps for Black to fall into, and most players today are not well-prepared to meet a Four Knights Game. To feel comfortable, the Candidate Master needs to know the Rubinstein idea for Black—3... Nf6 4. Bb5 Nd4!? The ideas are worth studying if only to eliminate the Four Knights as a dangerous weapon against you.

3... Nf6 4. d4

Now it looks as if we are going to have a Scotch Opening, but White has prepared a little surprise for us.

4... exd 5. Nd5

Moves like these can be very dangerous. Many times players find them in old and out-of-date chess books like Gossip's *Manual of Chess* 1880. They are not always easy to handle. Yugoslav Grandmaster Gligoric, in this position, played the inferior 5... h6 against Radojcic to avoid prepared analysis.

5... Be7

Calm, cool chess—the kind a Candidate Master might be expected to find. Black continues his development with no loss of time. Also playable is 5... Nxe4 which leads to an equal game by a tactical route. Black should probably be familiar with this one before trying it OTB.

6. Bf4

This is not the sharpest way to continue, but it should be good for equality. Up to this point, White had made his moves very quickly, using only a fraction of a minute for his first five moves. On the sixth move he used about five minutes to find 6. Bf4. The Candidate Master can be pretty sure, at this point, that White is out of his prepared variation–after one move! This is more common than one would think. White has probably prepared 5. Nd5 with only the tactical response 5... Nxe4 in mind.

6... d6 7. Qd3?!

This is a typical move of the indecisive. Keres analysed this position as equal after 7. Nxd4 Nxd5 8. exd5 Nxd4 9. Qxd4 Bf6= As a Candidate Master you must recognize this move as bad or at least inadequate. What is the best play against it?

7... 0-0

Straightforward and logical: the development looks like Black has paid the gambit Pawn, but it is White who has yet to regain it. How did this happen? White played an aggressive line (5. Nd5), continued tentatively with 6. Bf4, and now switches moods with the defensive 7. Qd3?! Logical, as noted above, was 7. Nxd4 (continuing to press forward).

8. Nxd4 Nxd5 9. exd5 Nxd4 10. Qxd4 Bf6

Diagram

Black has simplified the position in the center to gain the advantage of the occupation of the e-file. Note that Black is a full tempo ahead of the Keres' analysis.

11. Qb4 Re8+ 12. Kd2

How does Black punish White after 12. Be2 ? Although 12...

Bg4 does not win outright, prove to yourself that Black gains an advantage. Now how does Black proceed?

12... a5!?

Driving the Queen into a corner.

13. Qa3 Bf5

This is a good move. Perhaps a Master (or an annotator sitting at his desk) would find the win starting with 13... Re4 14. Be3 Bg5 15. Bd3 Rd4 16. Qb3 a4 17. Qb5 Bd7 18. Qxb7 Ra5! but this is very complicated and much more suited to correspondence chess than OTB calculation.

This developing move suits Black's general plan (which is?)– yes, pressure on the e-file against the King in the center.

14. Rd1

White is going to castle by hand–this would mean a disruption of Black's plan to bother the King in the center. Black sees a way to steal a Pawn. Black could also continue the attack with 14... Re4 15. Be3 Qe8. Which is the better course? It depends somewhat on your philosophy of chess. The Pawn is money in the bank, security for your old age. Quite a few things can go wrong, but that Pawn is real. The Masters will say, if you can't read the attack to the end, take the Pawn. This is how Masters play. But you are not a Master. You need to learn things Masters already know (That's why they are Masters). The player who wants to become an expert should pursue the attack. A possible conclusion could be 14... Re4 15. Bg3 (15. Qg3? Rxf4!) Qe8 16. Kc1 Rb4 17. c3 Bg5+ 18. f4 Qe3+ 19. Rd2 Rxf4!

**14... Bd4 15. Be3 Qf6 16. Kc1 Bxe3+ 17. fxe3 Qe5
18. Bb5 Qxe3+ 19. Qxe3 Rxe3**

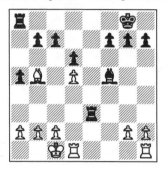

The nature of the game has changed. There is no more direct attack on the White King. An ending has been reached. Black has pocketed the Pawn. What should his long-range plan be?

20. Rhf1 Re5 21. a4?

A more alert White would have avoided the double attack by ... Be4 with g3, and a more prolonged battle would have ensued. Black's winning plan, a long one and difficult to put through without errors, is to queen the f-Pawn by operating on the Kingside where he has an extra Pawn. This plan, of course, is known to the Category I player. The precise execution of the play is known only to endgame masters.

21... Be4 22. Rfe1 Bxg2 23. Rxe5 dxe5 24. d6 cxd 25. Rxd6 g6

Taking care of business–the advance of the Kingside Pawns cannot be stopped.

26. Bc4 Bc6 27. b3 Kg7 28. Kd2 Re8 White Resigns

If you were playing White, should you resign? Only if you feel you could win with the Black pieces against anyone in the world. If you think Karpov or Kasparov might escape with the White pieces, do not resign such positions, in tournament play. Learn from your opponents' technique. Learn by formulating a play of resistance to see how it can be broken down. This is the cruelty of truth in chess: some positions are untenable.

1. e4 c5 2. c3

The Alapin Variation of the Sicilian. White does not wish to give up his d-Pawn for Black's c-Pawn. What is a good way for Black to continue?

2... d5

Black can also play the more positional 2... Nf6 3. e5 Nd5 4. d4 Nc6. With the text Black seeks an immediate fight in the center. Which method is more likely to succeed against a Category I player? That is not the question to ask. Which method best suits your style ? is the correct question. Find out the answer.

3. exd Qxd5 4. d4 Nf6

Usual is 4... Nc6 5. Nf3 Bg4 6. Be2 cxd 7. cxd e6 (why not Bxf3?–examine) Black tries something new. He avoids trying to conquer d4, probably a wise choice, and seeks flexibility. Would it have been better to have started with 2... Nf6, a more flexible choice?

5. Nf3 e6

In keeping with Black's intentions. Notice that 5... Bg4 would renew the fight for d4 at a time when Black is not ready for that fight. Instead he seeks early Kingside castling. Simple chess and good.

6. Bd3 Be7 7. 0-0 0-0 8. c4

Where does the Queen go? In keeping with Black's plan of flexibility, not 8... Qh5 but 8... Qd8.

8... Qd8 9. dxc Bxc5 10. Nc3 Nc6 11. a3

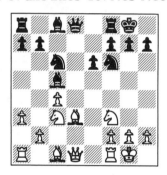

As a Candidate Master, how do you evaluate this position? What plan seems best? Why?

You undoubtedly saw the 3-to-2 Pawn majority for White on the Queenside. White's last move 11. a3 advertised it and announced his intention to advance it. Why is a 3-to-2 Pawn majority more dangerous than a 4-to-3 one? Answer: it can produce a passed Pawn faster. Two Pawn exchanges and a passer exists on the Queenside. Therefore the ending favors White slightly. The 4-to-3 Pawn majority means the existence of a center Pawn. If the center Pawn can be used effectively, attacking chances in the middle game will favor Black. Why?

11... a5?!

Although Black normally would not advance a Pawn on the side where White has the advantage, here he believes it will slow down White's advance. General principles should be violated only by direct calculation. The gain in holding back the Pawns for a few moves is lost in the quickness of the Pawn exchange occurring. Black might try 11... e5 or ... Re8.

12. Bg5 Be7 13. Bc2 h6 14. Bh4 Nh5?!

Black has played a logical game to this point. He could keep his aim for a Kingside attack by 14... e5 as 15. Bxf6 Bxf6 16. Nd5 Be6 17. Qd3 g6 and White may decide that 18. Nxf6+ is forced when 18... Qxf6 gives Black healthy play. Why does Black overlook this? Because he has looked at only half the problem–White's Pawn majority and did not take into account his own majority. Experts aren't Masters.

15. Qxd8 Bxd8 16. Bxd8 Rxd8 17. Rfd1 Bd7 DRAW AGREED

Draw?! You might wonder about this position being a draw. The answer of course is in that rating difference, here 125 points. White, being a Class A player, is content to draw against his higher-rated opponent. But you, look at the White side of this position. Would you give a draw to someone rated 125 points below you if you were playing the White pieces? Unlikely. If you have a slight advantage against an equal player, you also won't concede the draw. This expert used his rating to escape from a bad position. It's done all the time, but if you want to improve, fight these positions out. If you deserve to be a Candidate Master, you have to be willing to try to win these positions against your equals (Candidate Masters). White's try 18. Rd2 (the only open file!) Be8 19. R1d2 Rxd2 20. Rxd2 Rd8 21. Rxd8 Nxd8 22. Kf1 or 22. b4. The win is a long way off, but it is White who holds the advantage. Learning to exploit tangible advantages is a step toward rating improvement. Taking the draw in such positions is an admittance of being "only" a Class A player.

1. Nf3 c5 2. e4 Nc6 3. Bb5

By now you may be wondering about the unusual lines being played in the Sicilian. Master chess is full of theoretical lines tested over and over with improvements waiting on Move 23. These are the games published in most chess magazines, giving a false impression of the openings played at a lower level. There are several reasons that you will find unusual lines in the classic battles of Class A vs. Expert. First of all, tournament play, especially in weekenders, is practical play. Whatever works is used. If the Rosso-limo Variation of the Sicilian is not well-known by your opponent, it may bring in a full point. The ten thousand variations of the 3. d4 Sicilian are thus avoided.

3... g6

This is one of the good systems against the Rossolimo. Black generally wishes to avoid committing his center Pawns until White tips his hand.

4. 0-0 Bg7 5. c3 d6 6. Bxc6?!

White usually makes this exchange when he has a target for his pieces. Here the target Pawn, c6, is too deep into enemy territory for White to take advantage of. For this reason, the exchange on c6 is premature. As a Candidate Master you must now look upon the two Bishops as being a positive force in this position.

6... bxc6 7. d3 e5 8. Be3 Nf6 9. h3

This is a waste of time. Why? No Category I player playing for a win is going to decide on (without 9. h3) 9... Bg4 10. h3 Bxf3 11. Qxf3 or (after 9. Qd2) 9... Ng4 10. Bg5 f6 11. Bh4 with an advantage.

9... 0-0 10. c4

This is the type of move the Candidate Master always looks for, the positional weakening. What is a simple plan for Black? The Candidate Master sees d4 and figures out a Knight maneuver to get there. What is this maneuver?

10... Re8 11. Nc3 Nd7 12. Nd2 Nf8 13. Qc2?!

White, apparently, does not foresee Black's Knight maneuver, or he wouldn't place his Queen here where it will be attacked. White should undoubtedly have tried 13. f4. Black will continue his plan.

13... Ne6 14. f4 exf

The beginning of an ingenious, if not quite sound, attack. The positional continuation 14... Nd4 would increase Black's advantage, but the attacking line is good against Category I players who are, in general, poor defenders.

15. Bxf4 Qh4?!

Enterprising play–if 16. Bxd6 Ng5! and White is faced with a multitude of threats, but 17. Nf3 holds everything together: 16. Bxd6 Bd4+ 17. Kh2 Ng5 18. Bg3 Qh5 19. Qd1 drives back Black's attack. The conclusion? Though Category I players are poor defenders, it is still gambling to shy away from positional play. The gamble may succeed more often than not, but unsound play is still a gamble. Masters don't often gamble. Experts win many games against weaker opposition with successful gambles.

16. Be3?! Nd4

Black goes back to his positional plan, fortunately unharmed by his gamble. It is important that you see there is fear in White's heart. At this stage he is thinking he is lucky to be surviving. Such an attitude speeds defeat.

17. Qd1?! Bxh3!

This is no gamble–18. gxh3 Qg3+ 19. Kh1 Qxe3+ is the simplest method of defeating White. But here again we see something that happens time and time again like the snake hypnotizing the bird: the Class A player will not find the best line. Why? because he believes he is losing. He will not consider exchanging Queens while down a Pawn, but it is this plan that will make the resistance the greatest. The Category I player will miss 18. Qe1! and if 18... Qg4; 19. Qf2 with counterplay.

18. Rf4?! Qg3 19. Rf2 Bg4

The CM, however, strives to find good attacking moves everywhere. Not enough is 19... Qxe3 20. gxh3. He foresees 20. Qe1 Nc2 as being decisive.

20. Nf1 Qxf2+ 21. Bxf2 Bxd1 22. Nxd1 Rab8

With an exchange and an extra Pawn, Black has a technically easy win.

23. Ng3 Ne6 24. Rb1 Nf4 White Resigns

6

THE QUEEN'S PAWN

1. d4 d5 2. Nf3 Nf6 3. Bg5

You, the Candidate Master, can also play slightly unusual openings. White plans a Colle formation with the Bishop outside the Pawn structure, but mainly White plans on taking the Class A player out of his opening repetoire immediately.

3... e6 4. e3 c5 5. c3 Nc6 6. N1d2 Be7 7. Bd3 b6

Up to this point both sides have been developing logically, and one would expect to encounter 7... 0-0. The Candidate Master has two choices now–he can castle without thinking or try to plan a refutation of ... b6.

8. Rc1?!

Since plays like Qa4 or Bb5 lack punch after ... Bd7, any logical plan by White involves castling so White necessary moves first. Therefore 8. 0-0.

8... Bb7 9. 0-0 Qc7 10. Bb1

The normal procedure to get the advantage out of White's setup is to play e4. Can White play this? When the position of your pieces is all set up to play a particular move (e4), it should be played immediately or another piece should be played to support the move. Therefore White should play 10. e4 now, or play 10. Re1 or 10. Qe2. The play of 10. Bb1 does not help White's game in any way, whereas it may help Black to occupy the a6-f1 diagonal with tempo on the Rook on f1.

10... Nd7?!

White has shied away from e4, Black should castle. It is unlikely that White's attack will succeed down two tempi (Bb1 and Rc1). Why is Black afraid of castling? Because Category I players do not like to defend, and sometimes they delay "locating" the King before the opponent commits himself. If Black does not wish to defend, he should view castling as a preparatory move to the "attacking" ... e5.

11. Bxe7 Nxe7 12. e4!

Now White has come back to life because the two lost moves (Bb1, Rc1) have been regained by the two Knights moving from c6 to e7 and d7.

12... e5?!

What fundamental error is this Category I player trying? Yes, one that as a Candidate Master (think positively!) you will see immediately–Black is preparing to open up the center while his King is still in the danger zone.

> *The King sat upon a ledge*
> *Upon a ledge sat he*
> *He can go to the left,*
> *He can go to the right,*
> *Or he can set and let things be.*

13. dxe Nxe5 14. Nxe5 Qxe5 15. f4 Qf6?!

Naturally Black avoids 15... Qd6 as 16. Nc4 attacks the Queen, but a little more searching by the Category I player would have found that then 16... Qc7 is OK for him.

16. e5 Qh6?!

Black's Queen is misplaced on this side of the board. Better was 16... Qc6

17. Qe2 a5?!

Black pursues his King-in-the-center policy even though the center has become considerably loosened. Black should castle-either side, but he apparently can't bring himself to committing his King, not realizing how committal his play is.

18. f5 d4 19. cxd cxd 20. Ne4!

This move is logical and good. It involves a Pawn sacrifice that the Category I player will take. The tactics of Category I players aren't bad, but the timing often is. Black should castle now. Instead the Class A player gets brave and ends up in trouble.

20... Ba6?! 21. Bd3 Bxd3 22. Qxd3 Nxf5

Apparently well calculated by the Category I player, but the handicap of the King in the center is just too great.

23. Rce1

White can probably win after 23. Qb5+ but the text is devastating. The square e3 is protected, and if the Knight moves, Nd6+ is crushing.

23... g6 24. Nd6+! Kf8

Black can't try 24... Ke7 25. Rxf5! or 24... Nxd6 25. exd6+ Kf8 26. Qxd4 Qg7 27. Rf6! with an overwhelming game.

25. Nxf5 gxf5 26. Rxf5

By simple moves from move 12 on, White has achieved a

winning attack. Black's best is now 26... Re8, but White will still win
(Plan a win after 26... Re8).

26... Rd8? 27. e6! Black Resigns

7

THE ENGLISH OPENING

1. c4

You have faced an English before in this book where you essayed a gambit line. This time we will explore 1... e5. Obviously, this is a Sicilian reversed.

1... e5 2. Nc3 Nc6

Instead of exploring a wide open tactical line (2... Nf6 and ... d5), Black tries a quieter, positional line.

3. g3 g6 4. Bg2 Bg7 5. e3 d6 6. N1e2 N8e7 7. 0-0 0-0 8. a3

White finally announces his intentions of a Queenside Pawn advance. White would like to imagine he is playing this English Opening like Seirawan, but there are flaws in his setup. This frequently happens in English formations. The Candidate Master should know how to play the Black side of the English: center play to set up a Kingside attack. Black's play is standard procedure against White's setup.

8... Be6

Gaining time by the attack on the c-Pawn.

9. d3 Qd7 10. Rb1

Diagram

This is a wasted breath in White's Queenside attack. Black

could now continue 10... Bh3 removing White's best piece, his fianchettoed Bishop, which would be one way of beginning the attack on the White King. The removal of the Bishop on g2 leaves the squares h3 and f3 weak. Though this would be a typical way to continue the attack, Black elects for a Kingside Pawn storm, another good way to continue the attack, especially as White's Queenside Pawn action hasn't started yet.

10... f5 11. b4 g5! 12. b5 Nd8 13. a4 f4

Thus Black's attack arrives first with the threat of ... f3.

14. f3 Ng6 15. Ne4 h6 16. g4

White would prefer to play 16. d4, but the hanging c-Pawn makes this center play unpalatable.

16... fxe 17. Bxe3 b6

This is designed to prevent White's counterplay based on 18. c5, d5, c6! and Nc5. This action by White may or may not be a threat, but to avoid having to constantly calculate this maneuver in the pursuit of his attack, Black simply prevents this as a White option. This is not great chess, but it is winning chess.

18. N4g3

These are moves that signal a player's loss of will. White is retreating, regrouping defensively. There is no immediate need to rush to the defense. The Category I player might have shown some feistiness with 18. Rc1 to prepare resistance by d4. Failing to seek active counterplay means the Candidate Master has the opportunity to push White around.

18... Nf4 19. h3

Further indication of White's rabbit-like attitude. Even now 19. Rc1 was better as 19... Bxg4 is no threat–20. fxg4 Qxg4 21. Nxf4 Qxd1 22. Rbxd1 exf4 23. Bxa8 wins. What is happening here is an attitude question–the Class A player believes he is being beaten and is playing like he is–a fatal state of mind. Until you can calculate that you are losing, you should not *believe* you are being beaten (a very hard lesson to learn).

19... Nf7

Where is this Knight heading?

20 Bc1 Nh8!? 21. Nxf4?!

A further example of the defeatist attitude. Black's pieces are freed by this exchange–the Bishop on g7 comes alive and the Knight gains e5. Why does White allow this? because he believes he is losing, he is losing.

21... exf4 22. Ne2

More passive play. Notice that once a certain mental set strikes a player how most of his moves reflect that set.

22... Ng6 23. Bb2 Ne5 24. Nd4 Bf7

Black is still "playing positional" but he could activate his heavy pieces by 24... Rae8 25. Nxe6 Rxe6 26. Re1 R8e8 with the advantage. The text saves the white-squared Bishop but allows the further Knight invasion.

25. Nf5 Bg6 26. Nxg7 Qxg7

Diagram

White's spurt of activity began with 24. Nd4 has come to a rapid end. This is always that way it should be when an opponent plays with one active piece against an active enemy army. Black has conducted his game with quiet but forwardgoing moves. White's

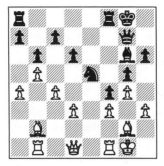

moves were a pot-pourri of defensive and active play. Net result: White's position is almost totally passive.

27. Bxe5

Or else the d-Pawn falls for free.

27... Qxe5 28. d4?

This error effectively ends the fight. Why does the blunder occur? One reason is simply the constant pressure White has been under. Such pressure creates its own blunders.

28... Qe3+ 29. Kh2 Bxb1 30. Qxb1 Qxd4

Preventing the perpetual check and stealing a Pawn to make the win technically easy.

31. Re1 Qg7

Deduct points for overanxiousness by 31... Rae8? The Candidate Master knows that such positions do not have to be rushed. Solid, strong play will defeat White: in such positions this kind of play is called technique.

32. Re6

White operates with certain primitive threats that look like tough resistance but aren't really. As long as White's Bishop remains disguised as a giant Pawn on g2, White is not playing down the exchange, but he is playing down a Rook. It is still unlikely that White will survive, but he would have more powers of resistance after Bf1.

32... Rf6 33. Rxf6 Qxf6 34. Qe4 Rb8

No hurry but 34... Rf8 would have been more accurate.

35. Bf1 Rf8 36. Bd3 Rf7 37. Qg6+

A bad exchange in a bad position: White should know better but he has obviously allowed his emotions to dominate his chess. How does Black win after 37. Qa8+ Kg7 38. Be4? Formulate mentally a winning line. Did you choose a suitable line to meet White's counterplay of Bd5?

37... Qxg6 38. Bxg6 Re7 39. Be4 Kg7 40. h4

How does Black win after 40. Kg2? Answer–since he is a Pawn ahead, a properly timed Rxe4 will win easily.

40... Kf6 41. h5 Rxe4 42. fxe4 Ke5 43. Kg2 Kxe4 White Resigns

1. e4 c5 2. Nf3 Nc6 3. d4 cxd 4. Nxd4 Nf6 5. Nc3 d6 6. Bc4

We have seen this Sozin-like move in a similar position in Game One. There we noted the simple trap White (and Black) needed to be aware of in this opening. White takes care to sidestep that trap.

6... e6 7. Be3 a6 8. a3

In an analagous position, Fischer pinpointed a3 as a loss of time and claimed the whole variation based on a3 was bad. Does this mean that the line cannot be tried in weekend tournaments? Of course not. Fischer was playing other Grandmasters. At that (very highest) level of play 8. a3 was weak. Against an opponent rated considerably under Grandmaster level, such ideas may work very well (but be careful! Class A players can prepare openings very well if they know you play a particular line).

White's idea, of course, is that in the Sozin (without a3) the Bishop usually retreats to b3 where it may later be exchanged by ... Na5 and ... Nxb3. Now the Bishop can go back to a2 and avoid exchanges.

But if the line is reputed to be weak (or weaker) should White ever play it? That depends on the philosophy of chess that White follows. If chess is an art or a search for truth–no. If chess is a fight–quite possible. If it is a sport? The decision belongs to each chess player.

8... Be7 9. Qe2 Qc7 10.0-0

With the weakening of his Pawn structure, White refrains from Queenside castling. This would give Black a clear cut tactical plan (... b5 and ... b4 attacking the weakened Pawn structure) and is therefore avoided by the Candidate Master: never give your opponent an easy plan to follow, especially if the plan is good.

10... 0-0 11. Ba2 b5

With the Bishop secure, White can begin his plan to weaken Black's center by f4-f5. Black must seek to find counterplay against this plan.

12. f4 Rd8

Here is Black's counterplay–to advance ... d5. It is said of the Sicilian if Black can get in a safe ... d5 he at least equalizes. The key word here is *safe*.

13. f5 d5?!

Another recurring theme in Sozin formations is the proper way of slowing down White's center attack by 13... Nxd4 14. Bxd4 e5 15. Be3 Bb7 when Black has good chances with pressure against White's center.

Why should Black's ... d5 fail? White's lead in development and well-placed pieces make the move very suspect. The Candidate Master is aware of this, and he will try to calculate a winning plan. What is your plan?

14. fxe

Obviously, if a win is on the board, it must come by opening up lines in the center.

14... fxe

Though 14... Bxe6 is slightly better, White would win in much the same fashion after 15. Nxe6

15. exd exd 16. Rxf6! Nxd4 17. Bxd4 Bxf6 18. Bxf6 Qc5+

It was important in your calculations started on move 16 that you noticed this move. If you did not, you need more *practice* in calculation. This can be done by studying and then restudying a game where you know the winning combination. Trace the moves mentally–and trace the moves in the notes also.

19. Qf2 Qxf2+ 20. Kxf2 gxf6 21. Bxd5+ Rxd5 22. Nxd5 Kf7

White has combined to produce this endgame. Is it a win for sure? or a draw? The Candidate Master should assume that any ending where he has a solid advantage is a win and play it as such. It is time now to make a new plan. What, in its simplest form, is White's winning play? The answer is the extra Pawn (on c2) and that lead in development is still very real. A winning plan would be to move the King into the center to support a Queenside action (play on the wing with the material advantage).

23. Rd1 Be6 24. Nf4 Rc8 25. c3 Rc6 26. Rd8 Ke7?

Black should avoid the exchange of pieces, standard procedure in any Pawn down ending.

27. Nxe6 Kxe6 28. Rh8 Rd6

Black shows familiarity with one truth of Rook and Pawn endings—active Rooks are much better fighters than passive Rooks. The win would still be there after 28... Rc7 29. Ra8 Rc6 30. Ra7 h6 31. Rh7

29. Ke2 Kd5

30. b3

White keeps the Black pieces out. If a win can be calculated after 30. Rxh7, that would be the more precise play. The move 30. b3 avoids the necessity of calculation. It is not art, but it is effective.

30... Re6+ 31. Kd3

In keeping with White's strategy 31. Kd2 would be more consistent.

31... Re1 32. Rxh7 Ra1 33. Rh5+ Kc6
34. Rf5 Rxa3 35. Rxf6+ Kb7 36. b4

Thus White has achieved an ending that most Class C players could win against a Category I player.

36... Ra2 37. Rg6 Rf2 38. h4 Rf4 39. h5 Rh4
40. h6 Rh2 41.g4 Black Resigns

1. e4 c5 2. d4 cxd 3. c3

Well, why not a Morra? The Morra is almost never seen in Grandmaster play because Grandmasters don't play 1845 players. But Candidate Masters do. An opening that may be poor against a Grandmaster can be excellent against lower-rated players.

3... d3

Black decides not to accept the gambit (see Game 45) and thinks that by counter-sacrificing the Pawn he can get equality.

4. c4!?

An important position for Morra players to remember.

White establishes a Maročzy bind. The Pawns on c4 and e4 make it very difficult for black to ever successfully play ... d5. If the d5 counter is denied Black, he may have difficulties equalizing.

4... d6

Black has the right idea but the wrong order of moves. He intends ... d6 ... g6 ... Bg7 ... Nf6 and ... 0-0 with a playable game, but 4... g6 first was better.

5. b3!? Nf6 6. Bxd3 Nc6

Notice how the Candidate Master is more familiar with how to handle the position. He understands the nature of the Maroczy which is to restrain Black's game. There is no great hurry to attack the Black formation as the bind limits Black's options.

7. Bb2 e6 8. Ne2

This is not accurate–not because White is going to lose the two Bishops but because the Bishop on d3 is not much of a Bishop. Also, when the Pawns are locked, as they are to some extent in the Maroczy, the Knights function very well–but because White needs to place pressure on d5 and Nc3 is the logical move. Later Ne2 or Nf3 may be better, but necessary or thematic moves should come first. It is not yet clear that e2 is the best square for the King Knight.

8... Nb4

One of the most difficult lessons a Candidate Master has to learn to master is how to obtain the two Bishops favorably. We can excuse Black's decision to go after the Two. Suffice it to say that 8... Be7 was better.

9. 0-0 Be7 10. N1c3 Nxd3 11. Qxd3 0-0

White needs to plan his continuation.

Diagram

The basic plan of the Maroczy bind holds true here–the d-Pawn is weak and cannot advance. Therefore White can choose several plans–Pawn breaks by c5 (even–observe the Pawn structure after the White c-Pawn and Black d-Pawn are removed), e5 (roughly even), f4-f5 (advantageous for White as ... e5 leaves d5 weak and

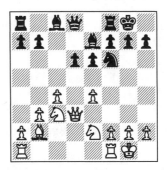

exf5 leaves the d-Pawn naked).

Therefore White will eventually play for f4-f5. First however, he should pile up on the d-Pawn to force Black on the defensive as defensive pieces don't have the mobility of free pieces. Therefore–White's plan should be Rad1, Kh1 (off the g1-a7 diagonal), f4, Ng3 and now f5 with the better game.

12. Rad1 Bd7 13. Qg3

This move looks good, attacking g7 and d6 and preparing to double on the d-file. It will cause Black to have to consider more defensive lines and use more time on the clock, if nothing else.

13... Rc8 14. Ba3?!

But this is ill-timed. Better was 14. Rd2 when f4 will allow the Rooks to join on the d-file or f-file.

14... Ne8 15. Bb2

Getting back on track, but it allows Black to rearrange his pieces to better defend. Such loss of time in a closed position is often not serious and occasionally is beneficial (gives the opponent a chance to make a mistake), but it does advertise a lack of understanding of the nature of the position. This gives confidence to the opponent.

15... Bf6 16. f4 Qc7 17. Kh1 a6 18. f5

White is still attacking–a strategy that we have found to be quite successful against Category I players. One drawback to f5 is that the square e5 is open, but Black will find it difficult to take advantage of this square.

18... b5!

Instead Black chips away at the Maroczy bind. When the c4 Pawn disappears, as it must here, Black's game will be a lot easier.

19. cxb axb 20. Nd4 Qa7

This double attack on d4 and a2 gives Black the advantage. The wasted tempi by Ba3-b2 has come back to haunt White, but Candidate Masters do not just lay down and die. White finds an intriguing resource, intriguing but unsound.

21. Ncxb5 Qxa2 22. Qf2?!

Was this an oversight (threat Ra1) or part of a deep tactical try? The Candidate Master should learn the value of the poker face. Don't give your opponent relief from his own doubt. By keeping one's expression confident, even if you see his win, the opponent is never sure whether the move is an error or a deeply laid trap. More than a few games have been won by a firm and strong hand.

22... Bxb5 23. e5!?

White understands well that 23. Nxb5 Qxb2 wins easily for Black. The move tried in the game should lose. You, as a student of chess, can analyse the win for Black–it is not too hard in the quiet of your study. But with the chess clock ticking and the nerves jumping, under tournament conditions, such moves are hard to meet. No one should desire getting into such positions as White–but once there, the expert digs in to fight the good fight.

23... Bxe5 24. fxe

Part of White's plan–the Pawn is immune and e7 is threatened.

24... Nf6

Did you analyse Black's win?

25. exf+ Rxf7 26. Rc1 Rcf8 27. Ra1 Bxd4
28. Qxd4 Qxb3 29. Rf3 Qc4 30. Qxd6

What happens next happens much too often to be chance.

Study the board. Who is winning? What is a winning plan? What can be done against the plan? Remember, the clock is ticking—there are still ten moves to go to time control though neither side really has to be overly concerned with the clock...

30... Ne4 31. Rxf7!

Time is ticking. After 31... Nxd6; 32. Rxg7+ Kh8 33. Rg6+ leads to mate. Black has to find a move–a man surprised is half beaten–and plays:

31... Rxf7? 32. Ra8+ Black Resigns

Black missed an easy win by 31... Qxf7. The question is why? Why is it that this kind of error is made more by the Category I player than the expert? Part of the answer is excitement. It is more exciting to beat someone rated above you than someone rated below you. It is necessary to control those emotions, to use them, to direct them. The expert about to be defeated knows the emotions in the Category I player and takes advantage of them by bringing doubt (complications) to the Class A player's game–if he can. It is under these conditions that many a winning game has been lost–a man surprised is half beaten. It is not esthetically pleasing chess, but the +1 on the scoreboard looks the same as the game won in brilliant fashion.

How can you, the reader, control your nerves? *I don't know.* That is something *you* need to find out.

1. d4 Nf6 2. Bf4

Now would you really play such a move? Alexander Alekhine once wrote that any opening is good enough if its reputation is bad enough. He was referring, of course, to the element of surprise in playing a "bad"-unpopular-opening. Actually, by making this move White can tell a lot about his opponent.

2... d5

If Black had tried 2... d6, White would have to be prepared to fight a different kind of game.

3. e3 e6 4. Nf3 c5 5. c3

This is the Pawn setup White was aiming for. It differs from Colle in that the Bishop is outside the Pawn structure (1. d4 d5 2. c4 e6 3. Nf3 Nf6 4. e3 c5 5. c3 Nc6 6. Bd3 etc.) Is this an advantage? disadvantage (Bishop is better on g5) or neutral-how can White use this Bishop advantageously? The expert should be ready to answer these theoretical questions. It doesn't matter so much what the answer is-chess can be a great ocean of ideas-the Candidate Master should be able to formulate an answer. Don't be lazy-go back and answer these questions.

5... Nc6 6. N1d2 Be7 7. h3

You have evaluated this position earlier. Evaluate this play.

What about 7. h4!? Obviously 7. Bd3 allows 7... Nh5. These kinds of positions are hard to judge OTB. One method is the belief of being the stronger player. Since development is equal, Pawn position roughly even, aggressive moves by White are unlikely to force the issue. Sound development to further control the center would be healthy. A non-committal move (7. h3 to save the two B's) is all right, but may hand over the first-move initiative to the opponent. Since White knows he is the better player, he plans to save the two Bishops for now and find winning chances later in the game. The above reasoning applies to 7. h4?! which the expert should reject.

7... Bd7

Sometimes moves like these are symptomatic of a lack of a plan. Is this the case here? The natural move was 7... 0-0. What should the Candidate Master do against an opponent who does not seem to have a plan? One answer is to improve his position but not offer his opponent a chance to make a logical plan based on his moves. Here White should complete his development and watch Black's movements.

8. Bd3 0-0 9. 0-0 Rc8

Now Black's plan–pressure on the c-file–becomes evident, but with the Pawn on c3, Black's Rook attacks a nearly unconquerable object–for now.

10. Qe2 Qb6

Aside from the fact that White's b-Pawn is attacked, this is a critical position in the game. White has developed his pieces and now has to think about his Rooks. Unless White can find some effective pawn moves, this is commitment time. The philosophy of "I'm the better player" can still be used–the game is still young–but generally should be set aside if a more aggressive continuation is available, i.e., sound aggressive chess.

11. Rab1

White probably has nothing better. To a large extent this can be traced back to 7. h3. Black has been making healthy developing moves–no obvious errors–so the inability to find aggressive play on move seven is reflected on move eleven. But White's position is fundamentally healthy, and being the stronger player, he has every reason to expect to win.

11... Rfd8

This is another critical position for the Candidate Master. All of Black's pieces seem to function together. White needs to find a way to use his Rooks as Black has posted his in potentially active posts. White undoubtedly looked at 12. Rfc1-d1 and -e1 but rejected them as basically meaningless so repositions his black-squared Bishop.

12. Bg5

Not bad psychology–White puts the onus of opening up the

game to Black. Not bad psychology but is it good chess? Category I players may be poor defenders, but they are good attackers, in general. The answer is, in this position, that attack is a long way away. White, being the better player, bides his time, not weakening his position, improving the placement of his pieces.

12... cxd

Black might have tried 12... h6 when the game might have taken on a different dimension.

13. exd a6

And now, once again, some major changes in the game have taken place. White's innoccuous moves–biding his time–have produced a position where he still has good chances. Notice that though "developed," Black's Rooks on c8 and d8 do nothing. This development, then, counts for little. White foresees a solid plan now–his pieces are still mainly Kingside oriented. After 14. Ne5 White threatens at least 15. Bxf6 Bxf6 16. Bxh7+ Kxh7 17. Qh5+ with an attack that will net a draw, minimally.

14. Ne5 Be8 15. Rfe1 Na7

Though Black is obviously now playing with a plan, he has begun to retreat over the board. This encourages White to become more aggressive.

16. Qf3

Siegbert Tarrasch used to comment that if he should lose his white-squared Bishop, he lost his Kingside attack. Perhaps a bit anthropomorphic, but the basic idea is true. Black's 15... Na7 is obviously designed to exchange Black's bad Bishop for White's attacking Bishop. White avoids the ripoff.

16... h6

General principles are ideas known to all of us that we violate when we have to. Though violated, they are still true. Black should not weaken his Kingside, where he is being attacked. The diagram shows the forces immediately involved on the Kingside. White owns a predominance of force.

17. Bf4 Bb5 18. Bc2

The Candidate Master notes that f7 is no longer guarded.

18... Be8

The Category I player does too-in effect, he passes to move. This is another critical point. In the play since move 10, White has done better than Black. Thoughts of a win should be on White's mind.

19. Nf1

The Candidate Master's solution-when the Knight enters the Kingside fray, Black will be dangerously outnumbered.

19... Nb5 20. Ne3 Nd6 21. N3g4 Nxg4 22. Qxg4 Kh8

Black's position is tottering—we see again the difficulty of the Category I player in defense–White, by avoiding hand to hand combat, has shifted the battle to where he wants to fight.

23. Qh5 Bf8 24. g4! g6!?

If the Candidate Master has only one specific edge over the Category I player, it would be that he plays better. This translates that he understands general principles better. We will not argue whether Black can survive White's attack. General principles tell us that ... g6 cannot be a good defense. All White pieces (except Rb1 and Kg1) are attacking on the Kingside. Black has Rd8 and Rc8 out of play. Therefore 24... g6 must help White.

25. Nxg6! fxg6 26. Bxg6 Bxg6 27. Qxg6 Nc4 28. b3

White would win after 28. Rxe6, but the text is efficient enough.

28... e5 29. Bxe5+ Nxe5 30. Qxb6 Nf3+
37. Kg2 Nxe1+ 32. Rxe1 Rd7

White has a winning game. The Rook and Bishop will be no match for the Queen and three Pawns. Nevertheless, White must win the game as Black is not going to oblige by resigning. The remaining part of this game is not art, it is butchery. But there is an art to being a good, efficient butcher. What is White's quickest winning procedure? If you selected Qe6 followed by pushing White's Kingside Pawns, you have talent to be a high-class butcher.

33. Qf6+ Bg7 34. Qg6 R7d8 35. Re7 Rg8 36. Rxb7

This Pawn has nothing to do with the game. This is a wasted move–better was 36. g5 with threats.

36... Rcf8 37. g5 Rxf2+ 38. Kxf2

White wins easily by falling into Black's plan.

38... Bxd4+ 39. exd4 Rxg6 40. gxh Rxh6

White has an easy win.

41. Kg3 Rd6

Once Black goes into passivity, the two Pawns will crush him by sheer gravity. Therefore, but also hopeless, 41... Rc6 to attack a2 or d4 should be tried.

42. Kf4 Rc6 43. a4 Rc3 44. Ke5 Rxh3
45. Kxd5 Black Resigns.

THE KING'S INDIAN DEFENSE

1. d4 Nf6 2. c4 g6 3. Nc3 Bg7 4. e4 0-0 5. Be3

White does not bite at 5. e5, whether out of fear or knowledge–this may be a sign that White doesn't want to be taken into unusual territory in the opening.

5... d6 6. Nf3 Bg4

Black is still looking to put White on unfamiliar ground. Against a Master, the Candidate Master would not play in this fashion. It is too dangerous, but he follows the philosophy expressed in Game 10. Notice, also, this attitude can do wonders against a booked-up Category I player.

7. Be2

A mild success for Black–7. h3 Bxf3 8. Qxf3 e5 9. Rd1 with the better position for White is an old analysis by Euwe. White's game is still healthy, but any book knowledge has evaporated.

7... Nfd7

A handy maneuver that King's Indian players should know. Black is going to conduct a Queenside attack so ... Nfd7 prepares ... c5, opens up the long black diagonal, and places another piece near the Queenside.

8. 0-0 c5 9. d5 Qa5 10. Bd2

The Bishop is not better placed on d2 than e3–this move is a waste of time as the Candidate Master demonstrates.

10... Na6!

A move that brands its player as a strong one. Most lower rated players–seeing that Bd2 indirectly attacked the Queen, would seek to safeguard it. The Candidate Master can *calculate* that there is no dangerous discovered attack and complete his development. Black's counterplay will be based on what?

11. a3 Bxf3!?

This is another move that speaks volumes about Black's understanding of the position. Study the reason for this play. On move 10 you were asked to consider Black's counterplay and no doubt you found a line somewhat like the game–... Rfb8, Qd8, Nc7, a6 and b5 with counterplay. If you noted that after ... Rfb8; Ng5! Bxe2; Qxe2 and with f4 to follow, White had strong attacking chances, go to the top of the rating list!

As it has been noted, Class A players generally are poor defenders but good attackers. To pull the claws from the lion before he attacks is good chess.

12. Bxf3 Rfb8 13. Rb1

This move violates the general principle of planning to open lines on the side of the board where the enemy is strongest. White could have given Black the greatest problems by 13. Bg4!? Qd8 14. f4 Nc7 15. Qe2 with attacking chances.

13... Qd8 14. b4?!

White is taking on several liabilities by this play, but he has committed himself to it. Now it is too late to switch to Kingside activity.

14... cxb 15. axb b6

Points to you if you see that ... b6 is not necessary and that ... Nc7 first would save a tempo in the attack. Once you decide on a plan, it is usually of paramount importance to be as efficient as possible in executing it. This efficiency, carried to its ultimate, is called mastery. Carried out to a high extent, it is the play of the Candidate Master. Here Black slips a notch.

16. Be2 Nc7 17. f4

Black has allowed this White move with tempo which makes his position more dangerous as the two Bishops might come to life, strongly, after a prepared e5. Better, however, was 17. Qc2 and 18. Rfc1! (Check this out).

17... a6 18. Qc2 b5 19. Be3 bxc 20. Bxc4 Nb5
21. Nxb5 axb5 22. Bd3

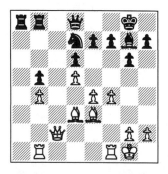

This is the type of position that separates the Candidate Master from the Category I player. Both players know that the two Bishops are valuable, but the Candidate Master knows how to use them (see Game 41, for example)–and play against them.

22... Nb6

Preparing to invade on the weakened squares on the Queenside. Obviously 23. Bxb5? fails to ... Nxd5!

23. Qf2?!

White had a difficult decision here–to play for a draw by 23. Bxb6 Qxb6+ 24. Kh1 when, though weak on the dark squares, he would have fair chances for a draw. White is still depending on his Bishops for more, but can't figure out how to use them.

23... Ra3!

Black does not suffer from the same problems White has. He doesn't have the two Bishops: he's got two Rooks, a Knight, a Bishop, and a Queen, and knows all of them are needed in the battle.

24. Be2

Weak in defense, he clusters his pieces together, methodically diminishing their mobility.

24... Na4

Invasion of the square-snatchers! Black aims for c3.

25. Bf3 Rc8 26. Kh1?! R8c3 27. Bc1?! Rab3
28. Rxb3 Rxb3 29. f5?!

White, who has allowed himself to be thoroughly outplayed, continually fails to find good defensive lines. This is mainly due to depression. The player who believes he is lost (or losing) will have little difficulties finding losing lines to play. Yet, see games 9 and 22 for examples of how the Candidate Master will squirm and wriggle and, somehow, avoid losing. Alexander Alekhine once remarked there was a period in his career where he felt that no one could possibly beat him. Only a few did, but what a positive attitude to have as he devastated the rest of the chess world!

29... Rxb4 30. fxg6 hxg6 31. Bh5

This is the best defense White could come up with–a paucity of ideas.Whereas Black has consistently come up with ideas and plans to further his game, White has played aimlessly since move 17. Even a bad plan is better than no plan at all.

31... Qe8 32. Be2 Bd4 33. Bxb5

This marks the end of White's attack and defense. Analyse out to a win.

33... Bxf2 34. Bxe8 Rb1! 35. Bxf7+ Kxf7
36. Rxf2+ Ke8 37. Rc2?!

After 37. Rf1 Nc3 38. Re1 Nxe4! 39. Kg1 Nc3 40. Kf1 Nxd5 and a Master will win the endgame. The Candidate Master will probably win the ending against a Category I player, but White has chances to survive. Now the game is over.

37... Nb32 38. Rc3 Nd3!

Busting White's (weak) defense.

39. h4 Rxc1+ 40. Rxc1 Nxc1 41. Kh2 Ne2 White Resigns

1. d4 d5 2. c4 dxc 3. Qa4+

As a Candidate Master you should be alert to more than just what goes on the chessboard. The move 3. Qa4+ is unusual. Was it played quickly, suggesting a prepared variation or after a normal period of thought, suggesting unfamiliarity with the opening? In this case White played 3. Qa4+ quickly. Plan a line against 3. Qa4+

3... Nc6!?

If you opted for 3... c6 4. Qxc4 Nf6 5. Nf3 Bf5, take full credit for transposing into safe and standard lines. Black's chosen line seems even better. Black plans to pester White's Queen with his pieces to gain equality–4. Nf3 a6 5. Qxc4 Be6 6. Qd3 Nb4 8. Qd1 Nf6 is one possibility.

4. e3 Nf6 5. Bxc4

This makes White's Queen move somewhat suspect. Black, of course, notes that 5... Bd7 fails to 6. Qb3 and 5... Qd7 is met by 6. Bb5 so he elects to play 5... a6 and ... e6 and ... Bd7. Here we see a violation of opening principles: make necessary moves first. 5... e6 is the necessary move and should be made first. Black no doubt was "hoping" to play ... e5 in one move, but hope chess isn't good chess.

5... a6 6. b4?!

Enterprising play by the Category I player. Such moves usually turn out very well or very bad. How do you assess this move?

6... Bd7

Playing against a Class A player, you should recognize that 6. b4 does not advance White's game very much. A little delving might have found 6... e5! 7. b5 axb! 8. Qxa8 bxc4 with excellent play and material compensation for the exchange. When a class A Player plays unusually in the opening, the Candidate Master has to plan to take advantage of those moves or he will find himself at a disadvantage.

7. Qb3 e6 8. a3

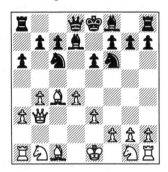

White's play has not been of a high order, but when Category I players play without the help of books, they do not play like masters, they play like Category I players. Black to play like an expert!

8... a5

Black, rightfully, plays to disrupt White's position, but even better would have been 8... b5! 9. Be2 a5! when White's Queenside play has led to Black's advantage.

9. b5 a4 10. Qd3 Na5 11. Ba2 c6

Black has started the war on the Queenside where he has an advantage. At this stage Black has outplayed White cleverly.

12. Nc3 Nb3

The attraction of catching the two Bishops has spoiled more games of Candidate Masters than any other strategem. But it also wins many games. Generally the chase of the Two Bishops is good play for a Candidate Master, but here it is not so good because Black has better than 12... Nb3. Analyze the possibilities of 12... cxb (opening up the position where Black is better developed) 13. Nxb5 Qb6 14. Rb1 Nb3 15. Nc3 Nxc1! 16. Rxc1 Bxa3 with a winning game.

13. Bxb3 axb3 14. Bb2

Now White is not too bad off. The Pawn on b3 is both weak and strong, and White has caught up in development. Black's plan for further play is?

14... cxb

Understandably Black wants to open up lines for his Bishops as Bishops are at their best when the board is wide open, but the power of the two bishops is that they can open up the lines themselves, later. The Pawn on b3, however, is Black's greatest worry. He elects to continue the immediate campaign to catch up in development.

15. Nxb5 Qa5+ 16. Nc3

Black has conducted the war in expert fashion. He now has to choose between 16... Bc6 17. Nf3 Be4 18. Qd2 and his b-Pawn is safe from assault and the aggressive 16... b5!? 17. Nf3 b4 18. axb Qxa1+ 19. Bxa1 Rxa1+ with a winning game. White may find a better defense, but this is the line Black should choose because it uses his b-Pawn, his most dangerous Pawn.

16... Bc6 17. f3

White tries to cross Black up by protecting e4 so Black continues to open up lines for his Bishops.

17... e5 18. N1e2 e4

Diagram

Black now enters into fuzzy ground. He has played well through-

out the game but begins to violate a sacred canon–opening up the game with his King in the center while the White King can escape by castling in one move. Though Black can often win material in such positions, the material won may not balance King safety. About equal is 18... Be7.

19. fxe Nxe4 20. 0-0 Nxc3 21. Nxc3 Qg5?!

Back is flaunting his King's desire to stand ground on e8. It is not too late for 21... Be7. Why is Black daring White? A little study would show that 21... Be7 22. Qc4 (Better than 22. d5 Rd8 when Black will be OK) 0-0 23. Qxb3 Qg5 when Black is better.

22. d5 Bd7

Now Black is forced to retreat–a bad sign against a Category I player. Losing is 22... Rd8 23. Qe4+.

23. Ne4 Qg6 24. Qd4

White disdains trying to win the b-Pawn. Now Black must concern himself with defending against Qe5+ Plan?

24... Rc8

While it is very true that Category I players don't defend as well as Masters do, Candidate Masters don't defend as well as Masters either. Black is counting on surviving in the center, but best was to offer some bait for White by 24... Be7 25. Qxg7 Rg8! 26. Qxg6 Rxg6 when Black has good chances to hold this Pawn down endgame. His Pawn on b3 is no longer weak, the a-Pawn may be hard to hold on to, and the King is no longer in danger.

25. Qe5+ Kd8 26. Rac1 f5

Black strives to drive the White Knight from the center. Though his game may be hopeless, the Candidate Master still strives to make the win difficult (or impossible) for the lesser-ranked player. If he is to go down to defeat, he tries to go down hard.

27. Rxc8+ Bxc8 28. Rc1

Well played. Analyse if 28... fxe4 loses.

28... Qb6

The Candidate Master sees that 28... fxe4 29. Qc7+ Ke8 30. Qxc8+ Kf7 31. Rc7+ Kg8 32. Rxg7+! Qxg7 33. Bxg7 Kxg7 34. Qxb7+ is hopeless.

29. Bd4 Qa5 30. Qb8 Ke7 31. Qxc8 Black Resigns

There are always lessons to be learned in chess–Class A players are dangerous. The Candidate Master cannot take them lightly. He must always strive to find the best line, attack or defense. Here our expert let the opponent off the hook. He began thinking defense from move 16 on rather than aggression, and then when the game began to go over to the opponent (moves 22 on), he could not find the best defense. Chess is a fight. Class A players will beat an expert who does not play well. It is not enough to be a good player–you must play well, too.

1. c4

Yes, this is the same player you faced in Game 12, but you are not the same player; you have learned something from that last game. A Candidate Master title is approaching the pinnacle of chess ratings. As mentioned before, a Candidate Master (2000) ranks above 93.9% of all tournament players.

An expert at 2100 ranks above 96.9% of the tournament players. You are right near the top. To fight against a Class A player, you must be ready to beat a Category I player who has beaten you before. Learn from your losses. Analyse–if you can, annotate them. You probably have a state organization with a chess publication. They need expert annotations. Send them some of your wins properly annotated, but annotate your losses, also, and keep them for yourself. And figure out where–and why–you went wrong.

1... Nf6 2. Nc3 e5 3. g3

Having been tactically outplayed in the first game, the Candidate Master is not afraid of outplaying his opponent in tactical play, but he also knows that tactically the Category I player is fairly close to him in strength while positionally the gap between the two is much greater. By avoiding "wild" openings as in Game 12, the Expert minimizes his losing chances. The question remains if he increases his winning chances.

3... g6 4. Bg2 Bg7 5. d3 d6 6. e4

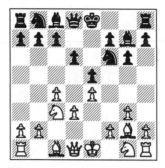

This is a difficult system, sometimes played by Grandmaster Ivkov. It is difficult because of the many Pawn moves White has at hand–b4, d4, and f4 are all breaks that may be beneficial to White at the right time. The drawback, of course, is the weakness on d4 and the slightly bad Bishop. All in all, this is a system that the Candidate Master can expect to play better than his Category I opponent.

6... Be6

A lot can be said about the attitude of the Black player even at this point: 6... c5 is an attempt to draw by symmetrical Pawn formations; 6... Nc6 would be an aggressive attempt to exploit d4; 6... 0-0 is non-committal, waiting for White to declare himself; and 6... Be6. Analyse for yourself the value (or lack of value) of 6... Be6.

7. N1e2 Nc6 8. 0-0 0-0 9. h3

Black has not coordinated his pieces well. The Bishop on e6 wants to support ... d5, but this is unlikely. The Knight on c6 would like to occupy d4, but this, too, doesn't seem good because 9... Nd4 10. Be3 c5 11. f4 and White has superior play.

9... Nd7

Not a bad solution to some of the problems facing Black–he can face the most threatening White lever–10. f4–by 10... f5 with sufficient counterplay.

10. Be3 a6?!

Diagram

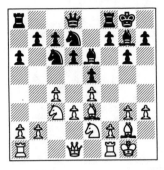

During the opening play, certain moves (f4 or f5 in this position) seem critical; they are balance moves. If White plays 11. f4, Black will respond ... f5 seeking balance. The Candidate Master knows that by keeping the "threat" of f4 in the air, Black has chances to go wrong.

11. Qd2 Rb8

White sees that continuing 12. f4 (which may theoretically be the best move) is not needed. Black is obviously planning ... b5. Construct a White play against ... b5.

12. b3 b5 13. f4 f6

Too late Black sees the point– 13... f5 cannot be played as 14. exf wins a piece. Now you have the Class A player at a serious disadvantage, both psychologically and chessically. He has had to make a distasteful move (13... f6). It is distasteful not because it is defensive, but because it forces Black to change his plans. Before his plan was clear: meet f4 with f5 and keep the center position roughly even, as both sides have the same number of pieces at roughly the same degree of influence. Now Black has to retreat, and this means he has to formulate a plan against a superior White center. This is difficult for a Master to do well, and almost impossible for a Category I player to do well. White needs to plan carefully.

14. Rac1

Not badly played. This may not be the best move in the position, but it is the move that most keeps Black fighting–he has to make some plan aginst White's overwhelming position. White should probably try 14. f5 Bf7 15. g4 g5 with some attacking chances, but it makes it easier to formulate a plan.

But chess is more than a simple slam-bam-attack-mate battle. Psychologists have their place on the chess board, too. The move 14. Rac1 is difficult for Black to meet: there is an immediate threat of 15. cxb, axb 16. Nxb5.

14... b4 15. Na4

White can also invade with 15. Nd5 as the threat of c5 is very strong. From a4 the White Knight reinforces the attack on c5 and White controls the entire board.

15... Rb7

An expert recognizes a move like this–the Rook uncoordinates itself with regard to the rest of Black's forces, a sign that Black does not understand the position. As a Candidate Master turn the board around. Put the Rook back on b8. What kind of a defensive plan can you come up with?

If you rejected 15... Qe7 because of 16. c5 with good chances for White, you probably thought a little deeper and came up with 15... Ne7 to meet 16. c5 with ... d5 and a playable game. This is the thought process you should use during a game to try to determine your opponent's best move. Variances from your opinion of "best" need to be carefully eye-balled.

16. d4

With this move White's clever strategy reaches a peak. By avoiding an immediate clash on the King's wing (14. f5) and the Queen's wing (16. c5), White dominates the entire board.This has not been accidental–it is the result of taking advantage of Black's inferior play and taking advantage of his befuddled attitude.

16... Nxd4?

It has been said before that it takes at least two mistakes to lose a chess game. Black has already made his share of errors. Plan a simple win.

17. Bxd4 exd4 18. f5 Black Resigns

White will end up a piece ahead after 18... Bf7 19. e5 with much the better game.

A good example of White's using Black's disturbed mental attitude against him to score a quick (and safe) win.

1. e4 e5 2. d4 exd 3. Nf3 Nc6 4. Nxd4 Bc5

This is one of the simplest lines for Black to try to achieve equality. More ambitious but equally sound is 4... Nf6.

5. c3

The expert should recognize this move as sound but very nonaggressive. White is quite likely already in unfamiliar territory. What is the best procedure when your opponent makes a passive move in the opening as White? This "error" in effect lets Black play the White pieces (White has lost nearly a full move with c3). Black should contrive to develop and pressure the White position. White's "error" hardly gives Black a winning game, only better chances for equality or a slight advantage.

5... Nf6 6. Nxc6 bxc6 7. Bd3 0-0 8. 0-0 d6

Not a bad move, but more like a "pass"–Black has played very simply, logically, and efficiently; White has wasted a move with c3. Therefore Black should press a little harder with 8... d5. It is impossible for the Candidate Master to fully calculate the resulting complications following 9. e5. Nevertheless, the Candidate Master will make this play more often than not as Black's game is better developed. Opening up the position and complications favor the better developed player, even if it is only by one move.

Some experts, though, prefer not to enter into unreadable complications, preferring to wait until they are sure they can beat their lower-rated opponent. Each school of thought has its adherents, but, unless you are strongly oriented to conservative play, the better results will be obtained by the first method.

9. Bg5 Rb8

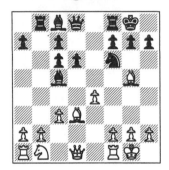

Black has to be careful here. White has a central advantage due to his Pawn on e4 vs. d6. Therefore Black needs to try to neutralize the center by putting more pressure there–9... h6 (to force the Bishop to h4 with less central influence) and 10... Re8 (threat ... g5) keeps White at bay.

10. b4 Bb6 11. Nd2

Now White is OK–the game is roughly even–notice how White has justified his 5. c3 by supporting b4.

11... h6 12. Bh4 Be6

Further central play–good for Black–and preventing 13. Nc4?! Bxc4 14. Bxc4 g5 15. Ng3 Nxe4.

13. Qc2

Diagram

These are critical positions–all the minor pieces are developed and the major pieces have to find proper squares. This is where the Candidate Master outplays the Category I player: the Category I player is still thinking development and material. The CM is thinking squares and mobility and, in the game, the two Bishops.

13... g5 14. Bg3 Nh5 15. Nf3 Nxg3 16. hxg3

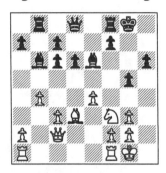

This position is an important one to note. William Steinitz, the first World Chess Champion, showed the chess world how to win such positions: two Bishops vs. Bishop and Knight, unbalanced Pawn position, Pawns controlling central squares to prevent the Knights from finding footholds there. It is worthwhile for the player who wants to be a Candidate Master to read Richard Reti's *Masters of the Chessboard* on Steinitz. Many games can be won by the two Bishops against the Category I player's Bishop plus Knight.

This is known as technique: the plan used to increase one's advantage in a general situation, in this case, the two B's vs. N+B, which is to keep the Knight out of the center, unbalance the Pawn position, create a passed Pawn, enter the King into the game, push the passed Pawn until it wins a piece or promotes. Then the "technique" becomes easier.

16... c5

Taking away the d4 square from the Knight.

17. b5?!

White, a Category I player, has not mastered the understanding of the two Bishop technique (keep the Knight out of the center) and does not find White's best– 17. bxc! Bxc5 18. Nd4 Bd7 19. Nf5! with fair drawing chances (opposite colored Bishops, the major defensive weapon in the Bishop and Knight's battle against the two Bishops).

17... c4?!

Not well played– 17... Qd7 with the idea of ... c6 seems best– Black anticipates White's plan of Nd2-c4 activating his pieces and prepares an attack on the White King. The power of the two Bishops, is the exchange of Bishop for Knight, is dictated by the possessor of the two Bishops, not the Bishop plus Knight.

18. Be2 g4 19. Nd4 Qg5!?

The square f2 will be hard to defend if White goes for opposite colored Bishops. The Category I player only has faith in the Bishops of opposite colors. The Candidate Master knows he can (possibly) attack f2 with Bishop, two Rooks, and Queen with good chances to break through.

20. Nxe6 fxe6 21. Bxc4 Qe5

Does Black have enough for his Pawn? Note that, at the very

least, defense by 22. Kh1 is met by 22... Qh5+ 23. Kg1, Qe5 = This is not particularly satisfying to the expert, but by this, he knows White's defense is very limited. Meanwhile, White must consider ... Qxg3.

22. Qd3 Kg7!?

The expert of course sees that 27.... Rf3 is met by the confusing 23. Bxe6+!? Black, being conservative, and enjoying the attack, is not about ready to let White off so cheaply.

23. a4 Rf3!

Now there is no confusion.

24. Qe2 R8f8!

Black has by logical play piled up on f2, and, apparently, suddenly White's game must fall apart. Check White's defensive plans. Defeat 25. gxf3 and 25. a5 and 25. Ra2.

25. Bxe6?!

White might have tried 25. Ra2!? for what it was worth. White's idea would be 25... Rxf2 is met by 26. Qxg4+ Kh8 27. R2xf2 with a winning game. The text is typical of the inability to defend of the player who believes he is losing. In order to do OK you must believe you are doing OK.

25... Qxg3

Plan Black's win after 26. Bf5.

26. e5 Rxf2 White Resigns

1. e4 b6 2. d4 Bb7 3. Bd3 e6

The player of the White pieces should know that the traps after 3... f5 are unclear: 4. exf Bxg2 5. Qh5+ g5 6. fxg Bg7 7. gxh+ Kf8 etc., but if White wishes to play conservatively after 3... f5 4. f3 leads to a good, solid game: 4... e6 5. Nc3 fxe 6. fxe Nf6 7. Nf3 with an edge according to Larsen.

4. Nf3 c5 5. c3 Be7

Better than GM Tartakover's 5... d6 as played in the Great Grand-father of this line in 1929.

6. 0-0 Qc7

White has to formulate his plans for middle-game play at this point. The position is worth a little study. White does not want to shut in his Bishop with N1d2 and is not sure where to place his Bishop-e3, g5, fight for f4, so he keeps his position flexible. Since he will probably advance d5 at some later stage in the game, White elects to play Re1 (overprotection–see Aron Nimzovich's classic *My System*).

7. Re1 Nf6 8. h3

Still temporizing, but 8. Bg5 was more active. In semi-closed positions like this one, it is not of great importance to develop quickly, but quick development is not usually wrong.

8... O-O 9. Bg5 d6 10. Na3

Superficially, this looks good, getting the Knight to b5 or c4 with tempo, but it is inferior to N1d2. After Black's ... a6 White will find it impossible to prevent ... b5. On a3 the Knight can go to c4 or e3 (via c2) while on d2 the Knight can go to c4 and e4 (after e5) or e3 or g3 (via f1) so the Knight stands much better on d2.

10... a6 11. e5 Ne8

Black, of course, does not exchange, but keeps the center flexible as possible.

12. Nc4 Bxg5?

Black errs–though he exchanges off one White piece, he brings a more dangerous piece to g5 and has to further weaken his Kingside. Better was 12... b5 with good chances of making a battle of it. The play 12... b5 is the logical follow-up of 10... a6 and drives a forward placed Knight away, relieves pressure on d6, and places the Pawn on b6 on a guarded square.

13. Nxg5?!

Diagram

Remove the Bishop on g5 and there are very few Candidate Masters who would refrain from 13. Bxh7+ with a winning attack. It is perhaps the automatic reflex to recapture material that causes White to avoid Tarrasch's good advice–"If you see a good move, sit on your hands! Look for a better one." After 13. Bxh7+ Kxh7 14.

Nxg5+ Kg6 (hopeless is ... Kg8; 15. Qh5) 15. Qg4 f5 16. Qh4 and Black will have to give up much material to prevent f4 and Qh7 mate.

13... g6 14. Qg4

White obviously has attacking chances, and Black has to find a way to survive. He would like to play ... f5 to allow his h7 square to be protectable, but 14... f5 15. exf Rxf6 16. Rxe6 wins a Pawn with a continuing attack.

14... Bd5?! 15. Ne3

This is not bad play. White can probably win by direct attack by 15. Qh4, h5 16. exd Nxd6 17. Ne5 Nf5 18. Bxf5 exf5 19. g4 with strong chances, but the Expert recognizes the Knight shift to the Kingside more than balances the Bishop on d5. The attack, then, continues, perhaps a little slower than the above line but practically as sure. Black has to find a defense even while White is, for the moment, threatening nothing concrete–not only distasteful but difficult to the Category I player.

15... c4 16. Bc2 h6?!

Greatly weakening g6: if Black is to hold this position, he has to get his Queenside pieces to the Kingside. The fact that he cannot do this is proof that the Category I player lacks defensive tools. The Candidate Master searches for an effective defense, one that allows all or most of his pieces to participate. The fault with ... h6 is that through it drives the well-placed Knight away, it contributes nothing to the future defense of the King. This is defense without a plan.

17. Nxd5

Of course the expert knows that 17. Nf3 Bxf3 would greatly diminish his attack so he saves the "better" Knight.

17... exd5 18. Nf3

Subtract three points for the overzealous 18. e6, f5. White goes after the weakened g6 square.

18... Kg7

Again, Black defends for the move only, rather than developing a plan to use his pieces–Nc6, e7 was Black's last chance, though even then the Candidate Master's attack will most likely triumph. It is extremely difficult to defend critical positions for several hours as the tournament clock ticks on.

19. Nh4 Rh8

Notice the futility of Black's defense. His defensive piece on f8 leaves for h8. Though h6 is guarded, the f-file becomes weaker, and g6, his weakest point, remains barely protected.

20. e6!

Now g6 decays and with it Black's game.

20... Nf6 21. Qg3 Nh5 22. Qf3

And now even 22... Nc6 fails as 23. exf Qxf7 24. Qxf7+ Kxf7 25. Bxg6+ is an easy win for White. The rest is just death throes.

22... Nf6 23. exf Ne4 24. Bxe4 dxe4 25. Qxe4 Black Resigns

16

THE DUTCH DEFENSE

1. Nf3 b6

In general, the earlier the Candidate Master can get his opponent out of the books, the better. Translated, this means the Candidate Master knows more openings and more opening variants. His play can, if he chooses, be more flexible. This knowledge comes from study, experience, talent, and a better general understanding of opening principles.

2. g3 Bb7 3. Bg2 e6 4. c4 f5

We have entered into a Dutch formation. This will be a double-edged fight involving the center squares e4, e5, and d5. That is why this position mildly favors White–two of the critical squares are in Black's territory and only one in White's.

5. 0-0 Nf6 6. d4 d6

Black avoids the superficial 6... Be7 7. d5!? exd 8. Nd4 with advantage to White.

7. Nc3 Be7 8. Qc2 Qc8!?

This is a good all-purpose move, shoring up the f5 and e6 squares, guarding the b7 Bishop; the tactical fact that White's Queen on c2 is not guarded vs. Black's guarded Queen on c8 is not lost to Black either.

9. Rd1 0-0 10. d5

White strikes before Black can complete his development. This is another moment in the game where the Candidate Master must make an important decision. The natural move seems to be 10... e5 and that move may or may not be played. Analyse the play after 10... e5. Then analyse other logical lines.

10... exd?!

In looking for lines, the Candidate Master rejects 10... Na6; 11. dxe and Black will have difficulties properly regaining the Pawn. He looks at 10... e5 (the natural play) and sees 11. e4 when White will gain the e4 square for his pieces–11... fxe 12. Nxe4 Nxe4 13. Qxe4 Nd7 14. Ng5 with advantage to White. He also sees that 11. Ng5 is troublesome.

But the Candidate Master should not be so quick to discard "ideal" moves. It is obvious that Black would like to play ... e5 if he can: 10... e5 11. e4 fxe 12. Nxe4 Nxe4 13. Qxe4 Qf5! offers Black his best chance for equality. White's game is only slightly better, and the unbalanced position gives the expert plenty of opportunities to outplay his opponent as the game progresses. After 11. Ng5 N6d7 12. Ne6 Rf6 Black will soon be able to drive the Knight from e6 without compromising his position.

11. cxd c6?!

This is all wrong–Black, whose pieces don't cooperate well in the center, who is behind in development, tries to open up lines where White is strong. Such strategy is not Candidate Master play–it is unlikely to befuddle a White player as Black's pieces are not aggressively placed. He is putting no pressure on White's game. Though Class A players are not good defenders, given the chance they can be excellent attackers. Black should be wary.

12. Nd4!

A devastating reply—Black must seek some method to keep his game intact. This is not a pleasant task, but sometimes chess is a tough, gritty game. Everyone enjoys attacking. Sometimes, though, the Candidate Master must defend, and he must defend as well as his position allows. Work on a defense—any defense that will slow White down—that Black can try.

12... cxd?!

Sometimes experts play like masochists. If you selected 12... Nxd5 to exchange a few pieces, bravo!—you are on your way to a Candidate Master's rating. If you foresaw 12... Nxd5 13. Nxd5 cxd5 14. Qxc8 Rxc8 15. Nxf5 Bf8 16. Bxd5+ Bxd5 17. Rxd5 Na6 and Black has some counterplay. The important part of the defense is another fundamental truth: endgames are generally harder to play then middlegames.

13. Nxf5 Re8 14. Nxe7+ Rxe7 15. Bf4

Here is part of Black's problem—by not exchanging any pieces to defend his King and center, he has fallen further behind in development. It is not enough, in defense, to just hang on: he must hang on and strive to keep his pieces active. The diagram here shows Black's flaws. He has defended like a Category I player, defending each threat in turn without trying to get all his pieces working together.

Black avoided losing a Pawn when he played 12... cxd (instead of 12... Nxd5)–but look at the Pawns he avoided losing on d5 and d6. Even now, at this late date, Black could try to confuse matters by 15... Ne4, but by steady play, 16. Rac1 Nxc3 17. Qxc3 Qxc3 18. Rxc3 d4 19. Bxb7 Rxb7 20. Rc8+ Kf7 21. Rxd4 White obtains an overwhelming advantage.

Why has the Candidate Master played so passively? Some defeats are necessary in any Candidate Master's career. The important matter is for the Candidate Master to learn from his defeats. You should analyse your losses, dissect them, and learn from them, but learn to apply the lesson in a *general* manner.

15... Nc6?! 16. Nxd5 Nxd5 17. Bxd5+ Kh8 18. Bxd6

By not surrendering the Pawn early, he has surrendered it late, and with interest. You must not underestimate your adversary. Weak play will be punished. The Category I player may also remember GM Tartakover's advice: the greatest sin in chess is to overestimate your opponent's strength.

18... Re8 19. Rac1

There comes that time in a game when you must consider resignation. Here is one such time. Though Tartakover (again!) said that no one ever won a game by resigning, there is sometimes a post mortem. If the Category I player asks "to go over the game," you should accept, win, lose or draw. By the same coin, if you play a higher rated player, one a category or more above you, win, lose, or draw ask for a post mortem. This is an excellent way to learn about the game. Remember, the two of you have been locked in a struggle of opinions for several hours. The post mortem may give you valuable insights into the game and the thoughts of both the higher and lower rated players. Hopefully, it may also deepen your understanding of the game.

If you don't turn down the lower-rated player's request for analysis, perhaps you won't be turned down when you play that Master! A lesson that some people never learn is that good things have a way of happening to people who do good things.

19... Na5

If you would like to turn to the next game, no one would blame you, or you can stay to watch how a Category I player can slay a Candidate Master given the opportunity.

20. Qxc8 Raxc8 21. Bxb7 Nxb7 22. Rxc8 Rxc8
23. Bb4 Kg8 24. Rd7

Everywhere Black turns, White's pieces are better–there is not even a chance for resistance any more. Black plays on, however, hoping for a technical slip from his less-experienced adversary.

24... Rc1+ 25. Kg2 Nc5 26. Bxc5 bxc5
27. Rxa7 Rc2 28. Rc7 c4?!

Some minimal chances of survival are offered after 28... Rxe2 29. Rxc5 Rxb2. White still has a win, *but*, White must know how to do it. Verbalize a plan to win as White from this position. Do you know how? Consult Reuben Fine's *Basic Chess Endings* or Paul Keres' *Practical Chess Endings* to find out how to formulate the winning plan if you can't verbalize the win.

Even at this late stage, the possibilities of a draw are still in this "hopeless" position. The endgame is the refuge of a defenseless King.

29. e4 g5 30. g4 Kf8 31. a4 Ke8 32. a5 Kd8 33. Rc5

Black's whole position is *en prise*.

33... Kd7 34. a6 Kd6 35. a7 Kxc5
36. a8(Q) Rxb2 37. Qa3+ Black Resigns

1. e4 e6 2. d4 d5 3. Nc3 Bb4
4. e5 c5 5. a3 Bxc3+ 6. bxc3 Ne7 7. a4

Book preparation is an important part of the Candidate Master's strength. Generally it is his obligation to be better prepared than his Category I opponent. This preparation does not come from study alone. Practice–tournament play and correspondence chess–is the main building block of this knowledge. One valuable way to increase one's opening knowledge is to annotate your own game after the tournament, with special interest on opening play. Most states also have a state chess publication which would appreciate annotated games for their readership. Since these annotated games are for publication, the Candidate Master should take pains to make sure the annotations are sound and accurate. Even without publication, annotation of your own games is an extremely valuable means to improve your understanding of the game.

7... N8c6 8. Nf3 Bd7 9. Be2

The study of openings reveals nuances that are not easily decided when the clock is running. Without this book knowledge, White might spend much time deciding between 9. Bd3 and 9. Be2. Master practice (which is ultimately what determines "book" lines has determined that 8. Bd3 is best met by 8... c4 with adequate play for Black. Normally White would want to encourage ... c4 but the tempo gain (Bd3 and Be2) is compensation enough.

9... Qa5 10. Bd2

One problem of being well-booked is that memory is sometimes a substitute for thought. Although 10. Bd2 is recognized as a known line in this position (depending on what opening books one owns), 10. 0-0!? as in Muir-Borek, Correspondence 1980-1 is an improvement. The c-Pawn is untouchable. Analyse for yourself that 10... Qxc3 11. Bd2 will win for White. It is important to think about, not just remember, the moves one plays.

10... f6

The Category I player has exhausted his memory store. Important to the stability of Black's center is preventing white's c4. Consequently 10... c4!? as in Stein-Uhlmann, Stockholm 1962, is Black's best chance for equality. White replies 11. Ng5 and the fight for the advantage continues. Now what advantage does book knowledge give the expert? He knows what Black should have played (... c4) and plays to forever prevent Black from getting this move in: the power of knowledge.

11. exf gxf 12. c4!?

Now Black must retreat and White will gain an advantage.

12... Qc7 13. cxd N7xd5 14. dxc

This move, which wins a Pawn, also follows the strategical principle of opening up lines to enhance the power of the two Bishops. White has used the better opening play to establish the better game. It is now up to the Candidate Master to translate this advantage into a win against the lower-rated player.

14... 0-0-0 15. a5

Notice how the Candidate Master uses his extra Pawn as an attacking piece. This makes the advanced c-Pawn more than an extra Pawn to be used in a remote endgame.

15... a6 16. g3 e5 17. 0-0 Bg4 18. Nh4

White has some defensive problems to solve before he continues his attack. He therefore elects simplification. This is a sound way of continuing–seek simple solutions. Black's "threat" of Nc3 is reason enough to avoid complications.

18... Bxe2 19. Qxe2 Nd4 20. Qc4 Qc6
27. Rab1 Ne6 22. Be3 N6f4!?

What does a Candidate Master do when he is hit with a surprise move? The answer is a difficult one to assimilate. In this case the expert has been having everything his own way and suddenly Black threatens ... Nxe3 and ... Nh3 mate. White must do more than just react to the threat–he must plan a defense. In this case the defense is clear.

23. Bxf4

White had to see that "defense" by 23. Qe4 fails to 23... Ne2+ 24. Kh1 N2c3 26. Qf5+ Kb8. Instead he plans his defense on simplification (extra Pawn) and a calculation that Black's counterattack can be overcome.

23... Nxf4 24. Rfd1!? Rd4?!

Solid defense is the best discouragement to an attacker: 24... Nh3+ 25. Kf1 Qh1+ 26. Ke2 Qxh2 27. Qg4+ Kb8 28. Qf3 (threat: mate) will win for White.

25. Rxd4 exd4 26. gxf4

And Black has nothing. White will win easily now.

26... Qd7 27. c6! Qg4+ 28. Kh1 Qxf4 29. Qe6+ Kb8 30. Rxb7+ Ka8 31. Ra7+ Kb8 32. Qb3+ Kc8 33. Qb7+ Black Resigns

1. d4 d5 2. Bf4

The very opposite of book knowledge: the Candidate Master deliberately throws both parties onto their own resources. Although this obviously favors the Candidate Master, the drawback is that it is easier (maybe!) for the opponent to equalize–but he must find his own way.

2... Nf6

Nobody can fault 2... Bf5, but oddly enough it has rarely been tried against the "Business Man's Opening." Why "Business Man's Opening"? because White does not seek to overwhelm Black in the opening but just develop his pieces for business as usual. Is this an innocuous opening? No–there is still poison there as this game illustrates.

3. e3 e6 4. Nf3 Be7 5. h3

Previously played was 5. Bd3 0-0 6. N1d2 N8d7 7. Ne5!? Ufimtsev-Serendenko, USSR 1970, with advantage to White. By the text move White preserves his Queen Bishop against ... Nh5.

5... c5 6. c3 Nc6 7. N1d2 Ne4?!

Such moves are either very good or very bad. The Candidate Master has to take time to decide which: Black violates a basic rule–moving a piece twice in the opening, but he occupies an important central square. Plan White's reaction after 8. Bd3 f5.

8. Bd3 f5 9. Ne5!?

By using the threat of Qh5+ and f3, White can "violate" the rule of moving a piece twice, too.

9... 0-0 10. Qe2

White develops, keeping his plans masked, but 10. 0-0 cannot be bad, keeping a slight edge for White. The problem with Qe2 is that f3, Nxd2; Qxd2 gains no time for White and an immediate f3 fails to ... Bh4+.

10... Bd7 11. Rd1!?

This move is tactically sound–the Queen is x-rayed through a very congested d-file. Black, if he is tactically aware, will seek to find a way to keep the d-file closed, with a continuing struggle. The fact that Black does not understand the significance of 11. Rd1!? is indicative of the Category I player's weakness in seeing "through" pieces, of visualizing the Rook on d1 "attacking" the Queen on d8.

11... Be8?!

"Saving" the two Bishops . . .

12. dxc Bxc5 13. Bxe4 fxe4 14. Nxe4

And White has won a Pawn. A simple combination? No, more the result of a logical plan by the Candidate Master and simple development by the Category I player.

14... Qe7

Actually this is a critical moment in the game. Black might try 14... dxe4!? 15. Rxd8 Rxd8 when he is behind a Queen and a Pawn for Rook and Bishop. This might be a viable line but is rejected because of 16. Qc4 when White is obviously winning.

15. Nxc5 Qxc5 16. 0-0 Nxe5

Black is operating on the theory that Bishops of opposite colors will draw; the Candidate Master is aware that besides the opposite colored Bishops there are two Rooks and a Queen and an extra Pawn on the board.

17. Bxe5 Bb5 18. Qg4 Qe7 19. Rfe1 Rf5

Black is seeking active defense which is the toughest but best way to defend opposite colored Bishop endings. The active pieces are easiest to swap off leading to a real Bishops of opposite colors ending.

20. Bg3

It is important for White to be able to resist 20. Rxd5?! Rg5. Analyse that White should not pursue this line as Black increases his drawing chances.

20... Raf8 21. e4!

Again notice how the Candidate Master tries to utilize all his pieces: 21. e4! brings to life both Rooks, Queen, and eventually Bishop.

21... dxe?!

The Category I player fails to defend: it is the same old song. Black would probably lose, though slower, after 21... Rg5 22. Qh4 dxe, but this was the best defense.

22. Bd6

Now Black's game falls apart.

22... Qf6 23. Bxf8 Qxf8 24. Qh4 Black Resigns

Black chooses to end the uneven battle at this point. This decision cannot really be faulted–White should definitely win, but Black should probably play on. Pieces are even, at least temporarily. The true expert, which Black is not, does not give up so easily.

As White you played very well in this game.

19

THE SICILIAN DEFENSE

1. e4 c5 2. Bc4

In the last game we saw that an expert can, if he so chooses, take the Category I player out of the books quickly and successfully. This is not the case in reverse.

2... e6

Cutting down on White's Bishop's diagonal.

3. Nc3 Nc6 4. d3 Nf6 5. Bf4 d6

Black's recessed Pawn center keeps White's pieces from open lines. White already has not handled the opening well–he should have prepared f4 to continue with e5 or f5 at the right moment to put pressure on Black's game. The Candidate Master is aware of Pawn structures and how to use them.

6. Nf3 a6 7. a4 b6

It is not necessary to speedily castle in such positions. With the center not likely to be opened quickly, Black can leave his King on e8 until he decides where it would be best placed.

8. 0-0 Be7 9. Re1 Bb7 10. Ng5

This is White's first attacking foray and shortly to be his last. Without adequate Pawn support or preparation, White's attack is doomed to failure.

10... Qd7 11. e5 dxe 12. Bxe5 Nd4

Black, on the other hand, centralizes his forces and keeps his position sound. This is one major difference between the defensive strengths of the Candidate Master and the Category I player: cohesive defense, pieces that work together as a unit.

13. Ne2?!

White looks to exchange pieces but goes about it the wrong way: 13. N3e4!? would be a more logical way of proceeding, perhaps with c3 in mind, or even Nf3 with further simplification, if necessary.

13... h6 14. Nxd4?!

White decides to pass on 14. Nh3 Qc6 when White can expect nothing but trouble in guarding his position, but 14. Ne4 is quite playable and White's game is not bad. Why does the Category I player overlook this defense? Part of the reason is fear–he, of course, sees Black's attacking chances but believes by exchanging a few pieces he will end the attack. What he does not see is a method of coordinating his pieces for defense.

14... hxg5 15. Bxf6

After 15. Nf3 g4 16. Nd2 White has some small chances of survival, but it is not likely that White would be up to the defensive task.

15... gxf6 16. Ne2

It is positions like these that are the expert's bread-and-butter against the Category I player. The technique of winning with the two Bishops is one that must be part of the Candidate Master's repertoire. Many games between Class A and expert are determined by the handling, or the avoidance, of these positions.

In the present position White's chances of survival are considerably reduced by the presence of Queens, the open Rook file and the soon-to-be-forced Pawn weakening around the King.

16... Qc6 17. f3 0-0-0 18. Ng3 g4!?

With the opening of the g-file, the end is simply a matter of crushing White's resistance. The expert plans a swift conclusion in these positions–no need in prolonging a game which might give the adversary more moves to escape with a draw.

19. Qe2 gxf 20. gxf

White should seek some slight consolation in an ending after 20. Qxf3 Qxf3 (Also good for Black is... Qc7, but he should play the Pawn up ending–unless he can *calculate* a win after ... Qc7. The Pawn up, 2 B endgame, should be an easy win for the Candidate Master. One sure way to master that particular endgame is to play it.

20... Rdg8 21. Rf1 f5 22. Qe3 Qd6

With this, the game is over. Black's task has been relatively easy in this game. This is deceptive. White chose an innocuous opening and Black rode roughshod over him. This is what a Candidate Master should try to do against inferior openings.

23. f4 Qc6 24. Kf2 Rxh2+ 25. Ke1 Rxg3!
26. Qxg3 Bh4 White Resigns

1. d4 Nf6 2. c4 g6 3. Nc3 d5 4. cxd

Players willing to play sharply should favor the exchange line in the Grunfeld. Players more disposed to a quieter game, willing to outmaneuver their Category I opponent, might try 4. Nf3.

4... Nxd5 5. e4 Nxc3 6. bxc3 Bg7 7. Bc4 c5 8. Ne2 Qc7?!

Now the expert detects a deviation from the book lines–8... Nc6, 8... 0-0, or 8... cxd. Here Black places his Queen on c7 too early. What can White do to show 8... Qc7 is premature?

9. Bf4 e5 10. dxe Bxe5 11. Bh6!

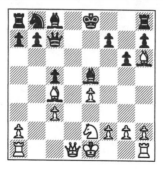

Black's game has become disorganized. Unable to castle, behind in development, one Pawn less in the center, Black's game is dangerously weakened. The expert should be concerned with increasing his advantage. A logical plan for White is: ?

11... Nc6 12. f4

White's plan of attack by 12. f4 and e5 is a sound one and should pay dividends by increasing his advantage. White's King-side Pawn majority can only aid his attack.

12... Bd6 13. 0-0 Be6!?

Black seeks to end White's direct attack by catching up in development and securing his King at the cost of a permanent weakness on e6.

14. Bxe6 fxe6 15. e5 Bf8

Black must take the opportunity to exchange pieces off.

16. Bxf8 Rxf8 17. Qb3 Qe7 18. Rad1

White, on the other hand, does not wish to exchange pieces, but that is what 18. Rad1, taking the open file and preventing castling allows. White's advantage is real, but he needs to act quickly: 18. Ng3 0-0-0 19. Ne4 was better play, and the attack would probably carry the day for White.

18... Rad8 19. Rxd8+ Nxd8

From here the Knight guards b7 and e6–and can go to f7 to protect a Knight invasion by d6. Only f6 remains critical. This gives Black chances to defend. One weak square can usually be tolerated, but once again the Category I player goes astray in defense.

20. Ng3 Rf7?! 21. Ne4 Kf8 22. Ng5 Rg7
23. Rd1 Kg8 24. Rxd8+?!
Diagram

White pays to cash in his chips, but by 24. Rd6! he can increase the pressure on e6 to an intolerable level. Black might try 24... Kh8, but White should soon win by 25. Nxe6 Nxe6 26. Qxe6 with good chances. The Candidate Master is guilty of forcing the game without taking into account a Black resource. Such things happen.

24... Qxd8 25. Nxe6 c4!

There are critical times in a game of chess. One of those times is when a player first realizes a combination has gone astray. The question then becomes one of how to make the best of a bad bargain. White needs first to get his nerves under control (if, as most chess players do, he has them). A technique used by a few experts that seems effective is to get up from the chess board, even though it is the expert's move, and go get a drink of water. Returning to the board, as near an objective approach to the position–i.e., calculation–will find the best move.

26. Qxc4

White avoids the shoals of the Knight vs. Rook ending by calculating that 26. Nxd8 cxb3 27. axb a5! 28. c4 Rd7 29. Ne6 h6! and Black wins by attacking b3. This is the strength of the Candidate Master over the Category I player. Given an inferior position, the Candidate Master will still try to find the best move.

26... Qd1+ 27. Kf2 Re7 28. Ng5+!?

White plays properly for a win–properly, but dangerously. Properly because the Knight and two Pawns are fully the equal of the Rook. Dangerously because of his King's weakness (if the d-file becomes open) and dangerous because an ending without Queens can easily be won by Black because of the weakness on the Queenside. With 28. Qc8+ Kf7 29. Ng5+ Kg7 28. Ne6+ White has a forced draw.

28... Kg7 29. Ne4

Spurning the draw again which White had by 29. Ne6+ as 29... Kh6 30. f5! forces Black to play for the draw. White, as befits his higher rating, wants to win very badly, but he must find a safe place for his King before he can try to attack Black again.

29... Qd7

Black retreats rather than counter threat with 29... Rd7. Note carefully the difference in attitude. Often the attitude of the Category I player is to regroup, defend, consolidate his position, and "try to win later." The Candidate Master knows the truth of chess that active pieces gain in strength. He tries to use the material he has immediately unless calculation proves it not feasible.

30. h3 b5 31. Qb4 a6 32. Nd6 Qa7+ 33. Kf3 Qd7

What did Black's last few moves accomplish? Nothing. White has been inching into Black's camp successfully and he should continue to do so with 34. Qc5. White has no winning chances on the Queenside–if he is going to win it will have to be on the Kingside and this means he must plan f5. This is best supported by a properly timed g4, obviously. Black should find defensive measures, but as we have seen so many times, Class A players defend against threats rather than plans. Analyse an aggressive plan for White.

34. Kg3?! h5?!

A move that is usually very good or very bad. It weakens the Black Kingside which is under siege (the squares g5, g6 become weaker and, by extension, f5). The only advantage is that it may prevent g4. All things analysed, 34... h5?! is a doubtful move, not a good one.

35. Qd4

The bad position of White's King prevents f5.

35... Qe6 36. Qb6?!

White is beginning to jeopardize matters if he goes after the Black Queenside. Actually he is anticipating 36... Qxa2 37. f5! Rxe5 38. Qc7+ with a White win, but White has not taken care of his King, and finally Black finds the way out and even justifies his 34th move. Analyse a better try for White.

36... g5 37. Qd8

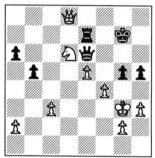

White's defense is based on a cheapo–Qxe7+ and Nf5+. Such defenses seldom work, though occasionally they do. The reason they seldom work is that they are directed against an attacker who has a choice of favorable variations. He is unlikely, unless exhausted by the pressure of the game, to blunder into White's trap.

Accurate calculation would lead White to play 37. fxg! although his chances of winning are nearly nil.

37... gxf+ 38. Kh2 Kg6?!

Befuddled by White's tactical defense, Black fails to find 38... f3! when Black still has winning chances. Why does the Category I player fail to find the best move? One reason is that he believes in

White's defense. The logic, faulty though it is, is that the Candidate Master is the better player; he will find the proper defense. So the Category I player believes White is doing well. This is an attitude that distinguishes the ranking of the player. The Candidate Master tries to analyse the position on the board, not the opponent.

39. h4 f3

Too late. Now the game dissolves into a draw. White's defense has succeeded.

40. gxf Qxe5+ 41. Kh3 Qe6+ 42. Kg3 Qe1+ 43. Kh3 Qe6+ 44. Kg3 Rd7 45. Qg5+ Kh7 46. Qxh5+ Kg8 47. Ne4 Rg7+ DRAW

The Category I player is occasionally an easy mark, but the major difference between the two is when the game takes an unsavory turn. At that time the Candidate Master digs in and strives to coordinate his pieces for both defense and offense, following the theory that since Class A players cannot defend well, counterattack is the best defense.

21

THE ROBATSCH DEFENSE

1. e4

The Candidate Master has to decide somewhere along the line about his opening repertoire. There are two lines of thought. One is to know a few openings very well indeed. The other is to try a variety of openings. There are advantages and disadvantages to both approaches. There is a certain strength in knowledge, a security of knowing not only the "best" opening moves but the typical middle game patterns, and in some cases, endgames that evolve out of familiar openings. The danger is stagnation and a deadening of creativity. To experiment is to learn, to find out always more about the game, to challenge. The danger is superficiality, and learning is sometimes a very painful–and discouraging–process. Each Candidate Master must decide for himself. Chess is a tough game.

1... g6 2. d4 Bg7 3. Nf3 d6 4. Be3 c6

Black chooses to avoid immediate contact in the center on the theory that the longer the superior player is flexible and avoids challenging White in the battle of the pieces, the better his chances to choose when to fight for an advantage.

5. c3

White, too, avoids direct piece play, working on the same theory. Here, though, the lower rated player errs. It is to the lower-rated player's advantage to confront the higher-rated player directly. This gives the Category I player the chance to shine tactically and overcome his deficiency of positional understanding. In a game between equal rated players, no fault can be found with 5. c3.

5... Nf6 6. Bd3

The first slip. The White Knight almost certainly should go to d2–the Bishop may have a choice between e2, d3, and c4–make necessary moves first!

6... N8d7 7. 0-0 e5

Now the Bishop on d3 might be preferred on e2 or c4. Chalk up superior opening play to the Candidate Master.

8. dxe

Another example of how, when faced with an unfamiliar opening, the lower-rated player may err, slightly, but err. The exchange negates the value of c3 protecting the center.

8... dxe 9. Qb3 0-0 10. h3

The expert knows that White has been mismanaging the opening. He also knows that because there is no direct clash of pieces he has, at best, only reached equality or a minimal plus over equals. Still, since the game is going his way, he should consider forward going activity with 10... Qa5 with the threat of... Nc5 gaining the two Bishops. Black's choice is not bad (10... Qc7) but the Candidate Master should look forward to positive moves once his opponent begins playing weakly.

10... Qc7 11. Na3 Nb6 12. Rfe1 Be6 13. Bxb6?!

After the more circumspect 13. Qc2, White is not at a disadvantage, Black's pieces not having any easy entry into the White position. Why then 13. Bxb6?! An attempt to question the motivation of one's opponent is sometimes commendable, but the Candidate Master must learn to be practical. When a move is made that is apparently bad, after analysis, he will find the good reply and not bother about psychological considerations.

13... axb6 14. Bc4 Bc8

Black is satisfied with the advantage of the two Bishops. In this position the advantage is only potential as the Pawn position is balanced and the doubled Pawns are of no advantage. Still the two B's are like money in the bank: later they will produce some interest. White has his own advantage: development. He should continue with 15. Rad1 with roughly even chances.

15. Qc2 b5

Proper technique with the two. Deprive the Knights access to the center, drive White's pieces into passive positions.

16. Bb3 Nh5 17. Rad1 Nf4 18. Ng5

White begins to flounder. He does not know how to make all his pieces cooperate. The expert knows he must find a plan for his Knight on a3. For this, as a Candidate Master, turn the board around. Find a viable plan for White to defend.

If you found the idea of Qd2, Nc2, Ne3, increase your rating.

18... h6 19. Nf3 Qe7 20. Re3

White fails to understand the importance of piece cooperation and wanders, planless.

20... h5

Black, on the other hand, begins to improve the position of his "bad" Bishop. Once Black finds a home for his light squared Bishop,

White's defensive abilities will not prove equal to the task. Once again the Candidate Master is in the process of proving the importance of technique with the pair of Bishops, a technique that must be developed for the Candidate Master.

21. h4?!

This frees the white-squared Bishop. The lack of a cohesive plan has transformed an equal position into a very difficult one in only three moves. This is not accidental, but typical of the clash between Category I players and Candidate Masters.

21... Bh6 22. Ng5

White does more than set loose a Pawn here. The Pawn position becomes unbalanced: Black's attacking chances increase. A solid defensive Knight is exchanged for a non-attacking Bishop. This is a further example of the lack of defensive techniques of the Category I player.

22... Bxg5 23. hxg5 Qxg5 24. Rg3 Qf6

Plan the attack. Notice that White is playing without his Bishop and Knight. Because of their noncooperation, Black should be able to force the win of more material or mate.

25. Qd2 h4 26. Rf3

After 26. Re3 Qg5 27. g3 Bg4 28. R1e1 Rad8, all Black's pieces are working. Plan the win.

26... Bg4 27. Rxf4 exf4

With 27... Qxf4 Black easily wins the ending. Black cannot be faulted for continuing the attack, but 27... Qxf4 is surer.

28. f3 Rad8 29. Qf2 Rxd1+ 30. Bxd1 Be6

Also good, of course, is 30... Rd8.
Now Black only needs to mop up, to be an elegant butcher.

31. Qa7 Qg5 32. Kf1 h3 33. gxh Bxh3+ 34. Ke1 Rd8 35. Be2 Qg3+ 36. Qf2 Qxf2+ 37. Kxf2 Rd2 38. c4 b4 White Resigns

22

THE BOGO-INDIAN DEFENSE

1. d4 Nf6 2. Nf3 e6 3. c4 Bb4+ 4. N1d2 c5

A little-known sideline of a little-played opening. White can almost certainly gain a slight edge by 5. a3 Bxd2+ 6. Bxd2 d6 7. Qc2 0-0 8. e3 with a sound position and the two Bishops, but in this position this is only a slight edge, probably just the advantage that White is entitled to as the first player.

5. e3 cxd 6. exd b6 7. a3 Bd6

The expert should be suspicious of this play. Though it attacks e5 and f4, the Bishop is somewhat exposed here. The main choices in the position were 7... Be7 or 7... Bxd2+ The virtue of 7... Bd6 is that it sets tactical problems for White to solve. The drawback is that, in general, the Class A player is better able to solve (favorable) tactical problems than positional ones.

8. Bd3 Bb7 9. 0-0 0-0 10. h3

Diagram

A temporizing move–White cannot commit himself to playing the logical 10. b4–10... a5?! 11. c5 Bf4 12. Nc4 with advantage to White. Also sound, and non-committal was 10. Re1 pressuring e4 and e5. This interlude gives the Candidate Master a chance to plan the further development of his game, but in viewing this position he should realize the awkwardness of the Bishop on d6. He can view h3 as a waste of time and play... Be7, placing the Bishop where it belongs, but, unwilling to admit the waste of time, he will play...

Nc6. Is there a safer plan?

10... Nc6

After 10... Bf4!? Black is not too bad off.

11. Re1 Rc8 12. b4 Bb8 13. Bb2 d5 14. c5 Nh5?

Stop! This move is, even without the question mark, obviously an error. What will White do? What should Black have done? Obviously correct was 14... bxc 15. bxc and then perhaps, ... Nh5. Why has a Candidate Master allowed this devastating Pawn advance? Part of the reason is psychological–Black does not wish to give White a protected passed Pawn on c5, but the fact of the matter is that the Pawn on c5 is already a protected passed Pawn. The Pawn on b6 in no way prohibits the forward march of the c-Pawn. The Candidate Master is planning a Kingside attack based on the sensitive f4 square, but he should first take the opportunity to blunt the White Queenside counterplay by paralyzing White's Pawns there. Now horrors await Black. Dig in, Candidate Master, for a hard game.

15. b5 Ne7 16. c6 Ba8

Diagram

The question of when to give up a piece for two Pawns or suffer passive defense and a shut in piece is often a hard one to evaluate. In general, it seems better to sacrifice–the active pieces that result

from the sacrifice help the superior player. The extra piece that comes as a result is not always handled well by the weaker player. In this and similar positions Black is already playing a piece down. The Bishop on a8 has only one future–to sacrifice itself on c6. There can never be a better time than immediately: Black has three pieces trained on c6. When, and if, White plays Rc1 and Ne5, Black may never be able to get two Pawns for his piece. Best was 16... Bxc6 17. bxc6 Rxc6 18. Rc1 Rxc1 19. Qxc1 Nf4 with advantage to White but Black has some chances.

17. Ne5 Nf4 18. Bc2

White is not defensive minded. This is a bad sign for the Candidate Master. White could have played 18. Bf1. The Bishop on c2 eyes Black's Kingside. Black has a large defensive task ahead of him–how to stop White's attack and how to play a piece down (Ba8). This is a heavy task. Formulate a fighting plan.

18... Nf5

Black might have tried 18... N7g6 19. Nxg6 fxg6 with some attacking chances as White's Bishop on b2 is not immediately better than the Black Bishop on a8.

19. Qg4 g5!?

The Candidate Master knows his position is critical. He is beaten on the Queenside. If his Kingside attack fails, he will lose. This, of course, is the fault of his fourteenth move. The Candidate Master is not usually a gambler. He prefers not to attack unless there is some real chance of success. He also knows when he *must* attack.

20. Bxf5 h5! 21. Qf3 exf5 22. Nd7

This is good play on White's part–key to Black's attack is the Bishop on b8. If White gets to play Nxb8, there will be little chance for Black. Black also cannot play 22... Re8 23. Rxe8+ Qxe8 24. Nf6+

22... g4 23. hxg hxg 24. Qe3 Bd6 25. a4

White delays taking the Rook on f8 as it cannot escape: 25... Re8 26. Qxe8+ Qxe8 27. Rxe8+ Rxe8 28. Nf6+ etc., with an easy win, but White should take the Rook.

25... Qg5

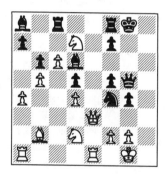

After 25... Qh4, Black threatens to get play with 26... Ne2+! 27. Kf1 Nf4 28. f3?! Rce8!? as 29. Qg1 is met with 29... Nd3 with an unclear position and after 28. Kg1 Ne2+ may draw. What can White do against the better 25... Qh4? 26. Nf1 is safe and sound, but then Black can try 26... Rfe8 giving up the two Rooks–27. Qxe8+ Rxe8 28. Rxe8+ Kg7 29. Rae1 Ne6! 30. Rxa8 f4 and the fight is not yet over. It is true that White will win in a master game, but this is not a master game. The expert's will to win is weakening. Discouragement over one's position is an easy way to find weaker moves.

26. Ba3 g3

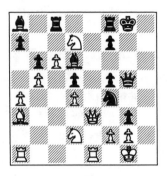

27. Bxd6?

This is a blunder and not a very subtle one at that. Why do such blunders occur and why do Candidate Masters profit from them more than Category I players? The answer is complex. One reason is a misunderstanding of the position. The offer of the Bishop on d6 should raise White's suspicion level. Another contributing cause is nervousness. The lower-rated player often gets his adrenalin pumping when he is winning against a higher-rated player. This nervous anticipation of victory has recorded many an underserved zero on the tournament wall charts. The same is not true of the Candidate Master playing a lower-rated player. This is one reason why the Candidate Master should not resign prematurely to the Category I player and why, especially in bad positions, he should steer for complications.

27... gxf+ 28. White Resigns

This resignation is also doubtful and illustrates more of what was mentioned above. After 28. Qxf2 Nh3+ 29. Kf1 Nxf2 30. Nf3 Qh6 31. Bxf8 Rxf8 32. Kxf2 White still has a winning game. Why does the Category I player gives up? Lack of discipline–depressed by the turn of events and the loss of the Queen, White allows his feelings to overpower his chess. Resignation is a very final act and should not be indulged in lightly. Here the Category I player believes he is beaten–he sees the high rating of his opponent and believes he will lose. Thus Tartakover's dictum: the greatest sin in chess is to overestimate your opponent. The Candidate Master knows he is a heavy favorite to beat the Class A player, and, most of the time, he does exactly that. Confidence is more than its own reward. The student who wishes to become a Candidate Master must develop a positive attitude: he must believe he can beat all the Category I players even if he doesn't. That belief will add many points to his score.

1. c4 Nf6 2. Nf3 g6 3. b4

In the battle between Candidate Master and Category I player, the Candidate Master holds many trumps. In general he has the better grasp of tactics and position play. In this game the Candidate Master announces his desire to outplay his opponent positionally. This is as good a method as any. The strength of a positional edge is that it will often survive a tactical setback.

3... Bg7 4. Bb2 0-0 5. g3

Continuing his overall plan, White avoids direct contact in the center. Some experts enjoy this method of play; some find it too slow, too devoid of the lust of conflict. All experts should be familiar with it and the strategic goals as they develop. They will either play it or play against it many times.

5... d6 6. Bg2 N8d7 7. 0-0 a6

Black falls into White's general strategy. The Class A player probably should not challenge the Candidate Master on the battle-field he has selected: better would be for Black to occupy the center by 7... e5 to intensify the struggle in the center with an increasing of tactical chances.

8. Qc2 c5

This allows White to achieve his first concrete step toward an advantage. He can exchange his b-Pawn for Black's c-Pawn and achieve a central edge.

9. bxc Nxc5 10. a4 Bd7 11. Nc3 Rb8 12. d3

The Candidate Master does not fall for the positional trap 12. d4?! Bf5! when Black conquers e4 and is in good shape. Patience and vigilance are required to play double fianchetto openings. Form a plan for White to increase his advantage.

12... Bc6 13. Rfc1

Key to White's plan would be the placement of his Rooks. For this purpose the b-file has to be paramount until other lines are open. For this reason 13. Rfb1 would be better.

13... Qb6

Another step–the Class A player begins to fade a little– 13... b6 with the idea of playing to support an eventual b5 would be safer.

14. a5 Qa7 15. e3 b6

Otherwise Black's Queenside remains paralyzed, but now the Pawn on a6 becomes isolated and weak.

16. d4!? N5d7

Of course 16... N5e4 17. d5 Nxc3 18. Bxc3 leaves White ready to invade c6 after 18... Ba8 19. axb Qxb6 20. Nd4.

17. axb Rxb6 18. d5 Ba8 19. Nd4

White has achieved his opening goal of a positional advantage, but now the game enters a tactical phase. The Candidate Master knows that the best way to fight a tactical interlude is to continue his pursuit of his strategical goal. If this entails a Pawn sacrifice, this is a small price to pay for a winning position. The key is for the Candidate Master to realize that he is winning–he has the better position. The attitude may not be all, but it is a lot. There is truth in chess: the inferior side should not benefit from tactical storms.

19... Ne5 20. Na4 Rb4!?

As the old writers used to say, the die is cast with this move. Actually White welcomes the opportunity to sacrifice a Pawn–all his pieces will come to life in the coming radical shift of the Pawn structure. His Bishop on g2 will soon become a powerhouse, the White Rooks will have open Queenside lines, and all his pieces will have squares. Finally the Pawn on c6 should snare something. The Candidate Master is on his way to a win. The Pawn on c4 is irrelevant.

21. Nc6!? Bxc6 22. dxc6 Rxc4 23. Bd4!

This keeps the most valuable Pawn on c6 well protected and seeks an exchange of Queens. Playable was 23. Qe2 but the text is sharper.

23... Qc7

Black cannot afford the endgame after 23... Rxc2 24. Bxa7 when the c-Pawn will net a full piece.

24. Bb6! Qc8 25. Qd2?!

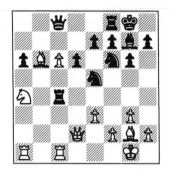

After conducting a fine game, White slips. Soon 25. Qd1! will win as Black cannot sacrifice the exchange by 25... Rxc6 as 26. Rxc6! Nxc6 27. Rc1 d5 28. Qc2 wins a piece.

25... Ne4!

Trying to turn the position around. Key now is to regain the thread of the game. Keep a cool head. You know how the pieces move–there are no surprise moves in chess. Formulate a defensive/aggressive plan.

26. Bxe4 Rxe4 27. Qd5 Qg4 28. f4

White needs to have carefully calculated this as his King's position is dangerously weak, but the Queen on d5 is ready for defense.

28... Nf3+ 29. Kf2 Bxa1 30. Qxe4 Nd2 31. Qd5 Qh3 33. Qg2!

And Black's attack has been stopped; the Pawn on c6 gains in importance.

32... Qxg2+ 33. Kxg2 Bf6 34. c7

After some excitement, White has realized his plans. Notice how a single-mindedness combined with cool calculated defense has led the Candidate Master to the verge of victory.

34... Rc8 35. Bd4 Bxd4 36. exd4 Nb3
37. Nb6 Rxc7 38. Rxc7 Nxd4 39. Rxe7 Kf8 40. Ra7

And White having reached time control, Black Resigns. This game typifies in many ways the difference in playing strength between Candidate Master and Category I player and is worth replaying. The astute student might try his hand at annotating it himself.

1. e4 c6 2. d4 d5 3. e5

White chooses to diverge from well-known lines and seek complications in lesser-explored territory. The Candidate Master should welcome this variance. It is easier to play against a Category I player than the collected wisdom of hundreds of Masters and Grandmasters (e.g., "book").

3... Bf5 4. Be3 e6 5. h4

White has found new territory–not necessarily favorable–Black has to meet the first threat in this game. What plan should be used to rescue the threatened Bishop?

5... h6

If you elected this play or 5... h5, you have let the Category I player gain a certain feeling of confidence. If you selected 5... Qb6!? you have the instinct to pressure Category I players. The Candidate Master should look for means to discomfit his opponent early–and by sound, logical moves.

8. Bd3 Bxd3 7. Qxd3

Diagram

Evaluate this position. What should Black's plan be? What weaknesses are there in White's position? What strengths in Black's?

7... Qa5+!?

This is an ambitious plan that pinpoints White's weakness: the Bishop on e3 and the white-squared weakness. The expert needs to be able to not only determine the flaw in the White position but how to exploit it. First analyse, then implement.

8. Nd2 Qa6 9. c4

Unwilling to acquiesce to the white-squared weakness, White is forced to go in for complications. The positional and tactical problems all favor Black. Why?

9... Bb4!

Further pressure on c4

10. b3?!

Now White has begun to think defensively. There is nothing wrong with being defensive when the position calls for it, but for White to have to defend on move 10 is often depressing for the Category I player.

10... Ne7

Now White cannot exchange on d5 for tactical (... Qxd3) and positional (... Nxd5) reasons. This means Black enjoys the option of exchanging. This tension hangs over White's head. The Candidate Master faced with such a problem will play to solve this dilemma. Since defense is called for, he will play Qc2, not fearing the "threat" of ... Nf5 and ... Nxe3.

11. g4?!

The White position is wide spread–he is striving for territory, but his pieces are not functioning well enough to hold all this territory. Retribution should not be too far away.

11... Nd7 12. Ne2 dxc!?

Black chooses this moment to cash in his positional chips before White can try Nf4, guarding his Queen and preparing c5!? with an equal game.

13. bxc

After 13. Qxc4, what is Black's best play? Analyze for yourself the difference in strength between 13... Qxc4 and 13... Qa5.

13... Nd5 14. 0-0 0-0-0!? 15. a3

This is part of the mind-set that White has been bullied into by Black's strong play. A stronger player might elect to sacrifice the c-Pawn and play for an attack against Black's King. This would certainly be the decision of a Master or strong expert, but as we have seen, Category I players can be beaten by their own play.

15... Bxd2 16. Bxd2 N5b6

Now the double threat of ... Nxe5 and ... Nxc4 will win material and White's pieces are not in attacking stances.

17. Qf3 Nxe5! 18. Qf4 N5xc4 19. Bb4 Rd7

Diagram

Black has established a winning edge. It is up to the Candidate Master not to let his prey get away. Lesser players often slack up at this stage, but the Candidate Master knows that there is much more to do. This "much more to do" is called technique. A more accurate term is *chess*. The struggle is not yet over. The expert has to put his opponent away.

20. Nc1

Threat: Nb3-c5 winning the exchange. What is Black's best?

20... Nd5 21. Qg3 Nxb4 22. Nb3

White plays on in hopes Black will become bored with the game and play... Nxa3 thoughtlessly.

22... Nd5 23. Nc5 Qb6 24. Rfb1 Qc7 25. Nxd7 Kxd7

There is no hurry to give White a little counterplay after 25... Qxg3+ 26. fxg3 Kxd7 27. Rxb7+ when the White Rooks are very troublesome. The expert must not play by rote. Many a won game has been spoiled that way.

26. a4 Qxg3+ 27. fxg3 Kc7 28. Kf2 Rd8 29. Rb3 Nf6 30. Rab1 b6 31. Rb4 Nxg4+ 32. Kg2 Nge3+ White Resigns

25

1. d4 Nf6 2. Bg5

This is bad strategy on the Class A player's part. The weaker player playing White has a better chance of gaining an opening advantage by playing book lines. The exception, of course, is if the Class A player habitually plays the rarer line. Then he gains knowledge, and knowledge is power in chess. The Candidate Master should welcome the opportunity to enter into little-known territory.

2... g6

Also good was 2... e6 3. e4!? h6 4. Bxf6 Qxf6 but the text move invites White to radically disturb the balance of the position, a goal of the Candidate Master in his attempts to win the game.

3. Bxf6

Thematic. The problem, of course, is that Black's position remains relatively flexible and the advantage of the two Bishops is a potential problem for White to solve.

3... exf6 4. e3

The leading exponent of this line tried 4. e4 against Eliskases in 1943 and equalized after 4... d5 5. Bd3 dxe 6. Bxe4 f5 7. Bf3 Bg7 8. c3 0-0. On general principles 4. e3 appears better as it does not open up lines for Black's two Bishops.

4... Bg7 5. Bd3 f5

Black clears lines for his black Bishop and plays to control e4.

6. Nc3

The first slip–White's Nc3 does not apply itself to the demands of the position. The c-Pawn is needed for proper control of the center. The square f4 is a natural one for the Knight so 6. Ne2 appears better. On c3 the Knight supports e4 which could have been played on move four.

6... Nc6 7. a3

White has forfeited his opening initiative. Why has this happened? Unless the aspirant Candidate Master has his Masters–in psychology–he should not ponder why. White is playing passively, and since Black is playing to win (facing a lesser-rated opponent) what is Black's best plan?

7... b6!

Although 7... 0-0 is logical 7... b6! has the advantage of placing the Bishop on a powerful diagonal at a time when White has adopted a passive stance. This is likely to produce further passive play on White's part. Alertness in the opening is a necessity for the Candidate Master.

8. N1e2 Bb7 9. Qd2

White continues dallying: a confusion of being unable to solve the problems of the position. Black, too, has a problem: what plan can he make? White's position, due to his defensive play, is very solid. Obviously 9... Qe7 has problems after 10. Nd5!? and 9... 0-0 commits his King. Black will play 9... Ne7 but castling may be better. Why? Why not? What is Black's idea after 9... Ne7?

9... Ne7 10. Rg1?!

The Candidate Master must recognize at this point that the Class A player's goal is a purely defensive stance: Do something to me. This is not a fighting attitude. To win, however, Black has to open up lines for his Bishops. What is Black's plan?

10... d5!?

Since e5 is under Black's control and e4 is, at worst, neutral, Black plans to open up lines by ... c5. Black is solidly outplaying White. The Candidate Master has taken control of the game.

11. Nf4 Qd7 12. Qe2

This is in keeping with White's passive defense, but White's tenth move, Rg1, has removed an important option: what is it?

12... 0-0

Since White can no longer castle Kingside, Black can ready a center attack or Queenside attack with the coming ... c5. White's passivity will soon prove his undoing.

13. g4

A futile gesture: Black has constructed a solid defensive position around his King by making aggressive moves. This is the strongest kind of defense. White's play is also typical of Category I play: an almost random mixture of attack and defense. White should, once adopting a defensive attitude, continue the same. These "attacking" gestures only succeed in loosening up his hard-wrought defense.

13... c5

Black uses his Pawns as a Candidate Master should, to open up lines to the White King.

14. dxc bxc 15. Bb5 Qd6 16. gxf Nxf5

The diagram is a good illustration of the result of White's mixing aggression and defense–little cohesion of the White forces. They do not work as a unit. Black obviously threatens ... d4 and there is little defense. White makes another typical error–not without its occasional rewards–and tries to solve his problems tactically. This violates another fundamental principle: tactics favor the player with the better position.

17. N3xd5?!

Analyse 17... Bxd5 18. 0-0-0 (or 18. Rd1).

17... Bxb2?!

This is an important lesson–the Candidate Master, knowing he has the better position, does not enter into unnecessary complications. He takes the safe line–but first he analyses the best line. Here he fails (but still keeps the win in hand). After 17... Bxd5 18. 0-0-0 Qe5, Black wins. After 17... Bxd5 18. Rd1 Nd4! 19. Qd3 Bf3, Black is obviously winning. These mental slips occur but the important thing is that the Candidate Master keeps his grip on the position.

18. Rd1 Bxd5 19. Rxd5 Qf6

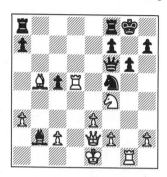

White's position is riddled with weaknesses. Once again the Candidate Master uses the Category I player's vacillating play against him. For better or for worse, for richer or for poorer, White is wedded to playing 20. Rxc5 when 20... Bxa3 gives strong play for Black, but the Category I player finds it very difficult to adjust his mental set (defense, passivity) to the changing position on the board.

20. Kf1?! Kh8?!

Why does the Candidate Master, in control of the game, make a move like this? The answer can be found in another book on how to become a Master. At this point it is sufficient to say that 20... Bxa3 is Black's best.

21. a4 Nd4!?

Black continues to present difficult choices to White. This is determination, and the expert recognizes this as "grip" or "the initiative." After 22. exd4 Qxf4 23. dxc Qxh2 Black is obviously better, but the fight continues. The Category I player, unlike the Candidate Master, rejects a line where he has a chance for a line that is unclear.

22. Nxg6+?! fxg6 23. exd4 Bxd4

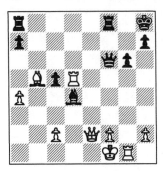

In this game of rapid see-saws, White had fought to a Bishop-of-opposite-colored position, but he remains defensive and this is enough for Black to formulate a win. This is not accidental.

24. Rg2 a6 25. Bd3?!

After this last defensive play, White is lost. The Candidate Master defending this position would certainly try 25. Bd7!? If Black can formulate a win after that, that is chess: the superior player deserves to win. It is difficult to change from passive play to accurate defensive play.

25... Rae8 26. Be4 Qf4

From now on Black has his own way.

27. Rxd4 cxd4 28. Rg4 Qxh2 29. f3 Qh1+
30. Rg1 Qh3+ 31. Kf2 Qh4+ 32. Rg3

A beaten attitude makes for an opponent's easy victory.

32... Rxe4 White Resigns

26

THE BENONI DEFENSE

1. d4 Nf6 2. c4 c5 3. d5 e6 4. Nc3 exd 5. cxd g6
6. e4 d6 7. Nf3 Bg7 8. Be2 0-0 9. 0-0 a6 10. a4

All this was played by the Category I player in one minute on the clock. Black, after his tenth move, had spent thirteen minutes even though the opening was just as familiar to him. Why the disparity of time? The Candidate Master knows he should not play by rote, to memorize an opening and mindlessly dash off the memorized moves. The problem with memory is that often the memorizer finds himself in a position, his memory bank exhausted, and he does not know *why* he has played the moves to get to this position. He must formulate a plan for the position he has attained instead of allowing the plan to develop logically and gradually from the flow of the position. Understanding of the moves is more powerful than memorization of moves. This is one of the arguments used against 5-minute chess, that it fosters such an approach to tournament chess. This argument is spurious if the tournament player doesn't forget and begin playing 5-minute chess in a tournament game. Very unlikely. the 5-minute games also give the Candidate Master some experience with a wide variety of positions and opponents, and, if used sanely, can only be beneficial to his game.

10... N8d7 11. Nd2 Re8 12. f4 Qe7

One advantage that memory does have over thought is memory doesn't even consider weaker moves. Here a "book" player would continue ... Rb8 ... b6 or the preferred ... c4 and worry later about how to react to White's next play. The disadvantage is that even a weak plan will beat someone with no plan at all, and the Candidate Master may not always find the best plan, but he doesn't usually find a weak plan, either.

13. Bf3

Why is Black's plan beginning with 12... Qe7 not good? Analyse the position. Why should White probably play 14. Qc2!? on his next turn?

13... Rb8 14. Qe2?! Qd8

Black finds it difficult to formulate a plan to integrate his pieces with the Queen on e7, so he undevelops to relocate it on c7. White proceedes methodically forward.

15. Re1 Nb6

Black finally works with a threat, but his Knight on b6 is misplaced. He needs a Pawn on b5 or b6.

16. Qd1 Qc7 17. a5 Nbd7 18. Nc4

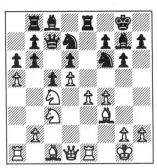

Black has to react in this position or he will choke to death. The Candidate Master is well aware of the freeing maneuver.

18... b5 19. axb Nxb6 20. Nxb6

The Class A player does not conceive the attack based on 20.

e5–a thematic idea in the Benoni. Here his memory has given him a false feeling for the position. An expert might well work out 20. e5! Nxc4 21. exf6 Rxe1+ 22. Qxe1 Bxf6 23. Qe8+ Kg7 24. Ne4 Be7?! 25. b3!

Often such chances are overlooked because the player who learns an opening by heart does not know the reason behind the moves.

20... Rxb6

Also good was 20... Qxb6 with the idea of ... Qb4 later and Queenside pressure.

21. Qc2 Bg4 22. Bd2 Bd7?!

Black changes his mind. *Why* is a legitimate question. After 22... Bxf3 23. gxf3 the Pawn position favors Black, the doubled Pawns being a drawback, only, to White.

23. Nd1?!

White is running backwards. His "threat" of Ba5 may be forward moving, but he is in full retreat at the moment, only one of his pieces beyond the second rank. Black could try 23... c4!? as 24. Ne3 fails to ... Nxe4! Black's next has all the ear-marks of a touch-move blunder.

23... Rb7? 24. Rxa6 Draw agreed

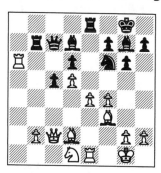

Why a draw? White has a free Pawn and no weaknesses of

great importance. The Candidate Master can "buy" these draws by virtue of his higher rating. Most Class A players, behind 300+ points in rating, are content to settle for a draw. The timing of when to offer it is important–the earlier the better. The second thing to remember is that the oftener you do this, the lesser your rating. It is usually easier to win an endgame from an even position than to win an endgame from an inferior position.

27

THE BENONI DEFENSE

**1. d4 Nf6 2. Nf3 e6 3. c4 c5 4. d5 exd
5. cxd d6 6. Nc3 g6 7. e4 Bg7 8. Bb5+**

One of the keys to improving to Candidate Master strength is to learn lessons from your games. This means work after the game or the tournament is over. In our previous game we saw 8. Be2. The Candidate Master has stored this information in his memory. Now he may be faced with a "new" move. Basically he is faced with three choices–8... N8d7 8... Bd7 and 8... N6d7. As a potential Candidate Master, what is your choice?

8... N6d7

Comment on this move.

If you chose this move over the other choices, you may suffer from something akin to the "horizon effect." In a similar position (1. d4 Nf6 2. c4 c5 3. d5 e6 4. Nc3 exd 5. cxd d6 6. e4 g6 7. f4 Bg7 8. Bb5+) 8... N8d7 is an error. The truth of the matter is that few players shy of some Grandmasters have encyclopedic memories that cover all openings. Black is suffering from residual memory. He recollects that in some variation (foggy in his memory but he suspects this is the line) that Bb5+ N8d7 (a logical move) fails to e5, with complications that favor White. Therefore he avoids both ... Bd7 and N8d7. This is the slavery of memory. The Candidate Master should be thinking at this stage rather than relying on quicksand memory. Score a minor victory for the Class A player. Is 8...

N6d7 a bad move? (though ... Bd7 or ... N8d7 may be better?)

9. 0-0 0-0 10. Bf4 Qe7?!

Does this fit in with Black's plan? Is 10... Qc7 better? As a Candidate Master you know that White plans to advance e5. To support this White will play Re1. Is the Queen better placed on e7 or c7 to hold back e5? Why?

11. Re1 a6

This is the flaw of 8. Bb5+–Black is free to either expand on the Queenside with ... b5 or capture the two Bishops. As a Candidate Master, which is preferable?– 12. Bf1 or Bxd7?

12. Bxd7?!

The Class A player cannot delve into the secrets of the position. Better was 12. Bf1 as 12... b5 will be met by e5 and White has achieved his break while Black's pieces on the Queenside remain entangled–13... dxe 14. d6! and d5 belongs to White–14... Qe6 15. Ng5! and the complications favor White–15... Qe8 16. Nd5 with the advantage. Notice how much better Black is with the Queen on c7.

12... Nxd7 13. a4

Restraint, but too late. Black has disentangled his Queenside. The position favors Black. Plan?

13... Rb8 14. Qd3

White uses his Queen to prevent ... b5. The Candidate Master recognizes that the Queen should not be performing such duties. He should recognize his advantage at this point: the two Bishops, the potential break ... b5 and White's e5 has been temporarily thwarted.

14... Re8

Nimzovich, in his book *My System*, an excellent text for Candidate Masters to learn from, would approve of this restraining move. Since Black cannot immediately play ... b5 he hinders White's plan of e5. Also good was ... b6 to answer a5 with ... b5. Black also has tactical chances based on a potential back-rank mate. Still,

Black would be happier with the Queen on c7.

15. Ra2

White, frustrated by his inability to play e5, adopts a defensive posture. This is not necessarily bad. Black certainly has played defensively, but 15. Rb1 accomplishes the same goal with the potentially aggressive b4 in mind.

This is typical of the clash between Category I player and Candidate Master. As the weaker player's aggressive lines are frustrated, he turns more and more toward passivity.

15... Ne5

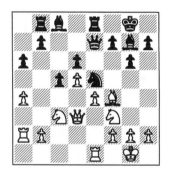

Though this surrenders the two Bishops, it frees his Queenside and conquers e5. The conquering of e5 will end up paralyzing White's Kingside majority. An expert with more patience would first play ... b6 to prevent the disruptive a5.

16. Nxe5 Bxe5 17. Bxe5 Qxe5 18. R2a1

White admits his error in 15. Ra2?! but such a candid attitude does not materially improve his position. White passes. It is now up to Black to plan to take advantage of his advantage. What are Black's advantages?

18... f5

Nimzovich (again!) verbalized how to attack a weakness: first create, then paralyze, then weaken, and finally conquer. The e-Pawn has been paralyzed—it cannot advance. Now it will be weakened. Obviously 19. exf is impossible. Analyse the flexible 18... b6.

19. f3

Here is the difference between playing a Category I player or playing against a Master. The Category I player has been beaten back consistently. He is not ready to realize that he can, though his game is inferior, fight aggressively. The e-Pawn is adequately protected. 19. a5 is still fighting (which is why Black's 19th should have been ... b6).

19... Bd7

The first move by this piece, and though it threatens ... b5, it allows White to fight on. Once again ... b6 is the right move. Why?

20. a5

This is necessary but not a success for White. The Queenside becomes roughly equal; Black takes an advantage on the Kingside despite his Pawn majority there.

20... b5 21. axb Rxb6 22. Qd2

An artificial threat of f4. White forces Black to make good moves.

22... f4

Evaluate this position.

23. Reb1

Now the Category I player elects to try to play on the side where you have the advantage.

23... R8b8 24. Ra2 Rb3

Black has dominated his opponent positionally. Already he threatens ... Rxc3. By all we have seen so far, the Category I player should fold shortly.

25. Nd1 Bc8 26. h3?!

Here is the beginning of the fold. White, not knowing how to defend properly, offers a target to the Bishop on c8. Though Black has the better position, can you find a plan of defense for White? Note that the Pawn position is roughly static.

26... R8b4 27. Kh2 g5

Signaling the final assault. The break by ... g4 should be decisive. If not ... c4 and ... c3 will prove decisive on the Queenside.

28. Rc1 h5 29. Nc3 g4 30. h4

It may well be that White is lost. A midnight analyst, postal player, or master will dig in and try to find a defense, partial or otherwise. The expert will enjoy the squirming of his Category I player (Bobby Fischer once said that what he most enjoyed about playing chess was to watch his opponent's will snap.) This may have happened on moves 25, 26, and 27.

30... g3+ 31. Kh1

No question mark though 31. Kg1 was better. As an exercise in calculation, prove to yourself that 31. Kg1 also loses. Do it!

31... Qf6 32. Kg1 Qxh4 33. Kf1 Qh1+ 34. Ke2 Qxg2+ 35. Kd3 Rd4+ White Resigns

1. e4 Nf6 2. e5 Ng8

Evaluate this move. The Candidate Master needs to approach the openings objectively. This move is both old and new. It was played by Flohr in the 30's and also, later, by Petrosian and Lein. As it is relatively unknown, the Candidate Master knows the Category I player will be thrown on his own resources.

3. d4 g6

Flohr tried the immediate 3... d6 against Spielmann in Prague 1930. Spielmann gained an opening advantage, but Spielmann was a Grandmaster. Your opponent is not.

4. Nf3

Boleslavsky played 4. Nc3 against Petrosian and Damski tried 4. Bd3 against Lein. The opening is little enough played that there is much room for new lines of play.

4... Bg7 5. Bc4

White loses a tempo by this move (see move 10) and allows Black to achieve an unbalanced Pawn position. This will cancel out the tempo lost by ... Ng8. What better piece alignment might White have tried?

5... d5

White has a critical choice at this point. The Candidate Master needs to mentally play both sides of the board. What is White's strongest play? Bb3? or exd? By analysing White's choices in advance, the Candidate Master can both save time on the clock and get an idea of how the game is going. White will play 6. exd. Why was 6. Bb3!? better?

6. exd cxd

If playing a stronger opponent 6... exd is more drawish, keeping the Pawn structure balanced. Against a lower-rated player, it is usually advisable to keep the Pawn position unbalanced, thereby decreasing the likelihood of a draw.

7. Be3

White continues a policy of development without a plan. Turn the board around. What better plan could White have? Is 7. 0-0 better immediately? Why? By working out White's best move, Black can often formulate his own plan.

7... Nc6 8. 0-0 Nf6 9. h3

Further passive play. It is time for the Candidate Master to make a plan for stealing the initiative away.

9... d5

Slightly better was 9... 0-0. White has not shown much desire to be aggressive with d5 himself. He has posted his pieces defensively, and gaining space by d5 may well rebound against him. Black plans to use the c-file to pressure the White position.

10. Bb3 0-0 11. N1d2 Qc7

A good move that Candidate Masters are on the look out for. On c7 the Queen begins the pressure on the c-file and keeps e5 away from White's Knight.

12. c4

Diagram

This is the typical error of the Category I player–he is more

likely to make a move "because it looks good" than as part of a larger plan. The Category I player sees Black's plan of pressure on the c-file and so advances to prevent this. White's play is not necessarily bad–he has left no weaknesses in his position until 12. c4. Passive play does not usually allow sudden aggressive plays. The Candidate Master has to know this and not be taken back by the apparent sudden shift of the game. Black may or may not have to shift his plan. What is Black's plan?

12... Rd8!

White is not prepared to advance c5 as Black has strong play after 13. c5 b6 14. Rc1 Ba6 15. Re1 Nb4 16. Ne5 Nd7! This comes about because of the logic of the position.

13. Qe2 Bf5 14. a3

White is returning to his passive play. Better was 14. Rac1.

14... Rac8 15. Rac1 Qb6

Black, who has conducted the opening quite well to this point, looks to clarify the issue by sacrificing a tempo. Sometimes this works out well, but 15... Qb8 accomplishes the same goal without allowing the complicating 16. c5!? The position is about equal after 16. c5 Qc7 17. Ba2 e5 18. dxe Nxe5 19. Nxe5 Qxe5 20. Nf3. This position, though, is unbalanced, and we would expect the Candidate Masters to play such positions better.

16. cxd?! Nxd5 17. Bxd5?! Rxd5 18. b4

White has continued his posture of defensive play, and the advantage has shifted strongly in Black's favor. Formulate a line to improve Black's play against White's weakest point.

18... Qd8!

Black exhibits an understanding of the position worthy of the Candidate Master. Once again the book *My System* (read it!) by Aron Nimzovich is a hallmark book on play against the isolated Pawn. White will find it very difficult to find adequate play for his pieces.

19. Nb3 e5!

Notice this position. The Candidate Master offers White the chance to dissolve his isolated d Pawn at the cost of Black's increased piece activity. White should leap at the chance but does not. This is because the Category I player does not fully understand the virtue of simplification.

20. Rfd1? exd 21. Bxd4?

Lack of calculation or desperation? It matters little–White would be lost after 21. Bf4 too.

21... Nxd4 22. Nfxd4 Rxc1 23. Rxc1 Bxd4 24. g4

Hanging on. Now Black has a new, and relatively pleasant, task ahead of him: technique. Winning the ending a piece up is a simple task, but it must be done.

24... Be6 25. Nxd4 Rxd4 26. Qe5 Rd1+
27. Rxd1 Qxd1+ 28. Kh2 Qd8

An overzealous Black might try for immediate mate by 28... Bd5 29. Qb8+ Kg7 30. Qe5+ when White's checks slow down Black's progress.

29. f4 a6 30. f5 gxf 31. gxf Qd2+ 32. Kg3 Qg5+ 33. Kh2 Qxf5
34. Qg3+ Kf8 35. Qd6+ Ke8 36. Qb8+ Bc8 37. a4 Qxh3+
38. Kg1 Qe3+ White Resigns

There should be no question in the Candidate Masters mind that Black should win.

29

BIRD'S OPENING

1. f4

As we have seen, Class A players frequently try to take Candidate Masters out of the book. This usually fails because of poor preparation: if the Class A player had studied and prepared this line, it might be a successful tactic. Here, as is usual, the Class A player is simply throwing both players upon their own resources, and the Candidate Master almost always has more resources to rely upon.

1... d5 2. Nf3 g6

One of several good methods to oppose the Bird's, Black contests the square e5.

3. e3 Bg7 4. c3 Nf6 5. d4 0-0 6. Bd3 N8d7 7. N1d2 c5

Black has equality in this position. White's plan to "confuse" Black by an off-beat opening has not succeeded.

8. b4 b6 9. 0-0 Qc7

With the threat of 10... cxb 11. cxb Qc3 winning at least a Pawn. Black has already begun to operate with threats. This is usually a sign that the opponent has not used his first-move advantage well.

10. Bb2 Bb7 11. a4

Black has completed his development–notice the superiority

of Black's Bishop on b7 to White's on b2. Black's Bishop fights for
e4; White's does not have any direct influence on e5. Black has to
find a constructive plan for his Rooks. Plan?

11... Rac8 12. a5 Ne4

Black begins central operations to offset White's Queenside
activity. The open a-file will not be wide enough for White to
undertake any significant action. The c-file will offer Black greater
scope.

13. axb axb 14. Qb1 cxb 15. cxb Nxd2 16. Nxd2 Qd6

Eyeing the b-Pawn and freeing the Rook on c8. Black has
accumulated some small advantages, but any win is still a long way
away.

17. Ra7

White fights well, trying to keep his pieces active, but once
again the lack of a cohesive plan is obvious: White is trying to solve
his problems one move at a time rather than find a comprehensive
strategy. This works, for a while, but eventually problems have a
habit of cropping up all over the board. A piece committed to solving a problem on one side of the board cannot always return to the
other side in time. Black will have to find a way to begin operations
on the Kingside.

17... Rc7 18. Rc1 Ra8

The Candidate Master must always be alert–the "natural" move
18... R8c8 loses to 19. Rxb7!

19. Rxa8+ Bxa8 20. Rxc7 Qxc7 21. Qc2 Qxc2 22. Bxc2

Diagram

The Category I player has defended well, swapping off the
heavy pieces, but now we arrive at another fundamental truth of
chess. Again, the old wisdom: "Most chess players play the openings like Grandmasters, the middle game like experts, and the
endgame like children." The difference in strength is magnified as
the pieces diminish. One reason for this is that, to get to Candidate

Master strength, some study of endgames is required. Certainly the fundamental King and Pawn endings, the two Bishops, and Rook endings should be part of the expert's repertoire.

22... Bc6

Black seizes the chance to activate his Bishop. Notice that a passive move like 22... e6 allows White to begin aggressive play with 23. Ba4. The position is still even.

23. Bd3 Ba4 24. Kf2 Nf6

Black again seeks to find better squares for his pieces. Black's King is not needed, yet, as White's pieces barricade his own King from coming to the Queenside.

25. Ke2 Ne8 26. Bb1 Nd6 27. Ba2 e6 28. Kd3?! Bf8

Black has made some progress since the exchange of heavy

pieces. Now he relocates the dark-squared Bishop attacking the b-Pawn. This also frees the King for possible action via Kg7-f6. White's 28. Kd3?! is bad because the King is not needed on the Queenside–28. Nb1!? is better (verify).

29. Bb3?!

White is headed for a blunder. Even without the blunder it is obvious that he does not understand the problems. The exchange of white-squared Bishops would favor Black; the exchange of White's dark-squared Bishop would aid White, even if it is for Black's Knight.

29... Bb5+ 30. Kc2 Nf5

Verify that White can take advantage of the inferior 30... Nc4?

Now Black is winning. This is the superior play of the Candidate Master versus the Category I player. By consistently improving the placement of his pieces, he has gained the win.

31. g3 Bxb4 32. e4 Ne3+ 33. Kc1 Nc4 34. Nxc4 dxc4

The two passed Pawns will be too much.

35. Ba2 c3 36. Ba1 Bd3 37. e5 Ba3+ White Resigns

A game that will benefit you by studying Black's sound, solid, and strong play from move 22 on.

1. d4 d5 2. c4 e6 3. Nc3 Nf6 4. Bg5 Be7
5. Nf3 N8d7 6. Qc2 c6 7. e3 h6

Black forces the Bishop to commit itself: 8. Bf4 Nh5!? This Rook Pawn advance has elements of weakness in it which must be carefully watched.

8. Bh4 0-0 9. cxd

White makes this exchange to lock the Pawn structure. It is easier to make plans when the Pawn skeleton is stationary. The drawback is that it is also easier for the lower-rated player to make plans also. Consequently, this is a good move for the Candidate Master to make against a Master but not so good against a Category I player.

9... Nxd5

Black, on the other hand, is happy to exchange a few pieces against his higher-rated opponent: the Candidate Master has released a lot of tension and Black is given an opportunity to simplify, making his planning of the middle game easier.

10. Bxe7 Qxe7 11. Bc4 Nxc3 12. bxc3 e5!

Diagram

Black achieves equality by this typical freeing maneuver. The opening has gone in Black's favor as the lower-rated player. The Candidate Master should recognize this and resign himself to castling. He is then ready to do further battle with an unbalanced

Pawn position, a situation that, in combat, would give the higher-rated player an edge. Instead he commits a fundamental error: entering into battle with his King in the center.

13. Qe4?!

Notice that this attack on the e-Pawn forces Black to develop his Rook while White moves a piece twice in the opening. White is making things too easy for his opponent by forcing tactics in a position where he can't properly bring more pieces (his Rooks) to bear.

13... Re8 14. Bd3 Nf6!

The Candidate Master is facing the Category I player at his best. He finds the weakness of White's strategy and takes advantage of it. This CM deserves this treatment–it is up to him to find superior plans in the positions that evolve on the chess board. Now it is up to the CM to reasess the position and find the way back into the game.

15. Qxe5 Qa3 16. Qc5 Qxc5 17. dxc5 Nd7

Diagram

Black has obtained the superior position. White has to plan how to play against Black's superior endgame. Why is Black's position superior? How should White play against it immediately? long term? Evaluate.

18. Rb1?! Nxc5 19. Bc2 Be6 20. Bb3?!

White is still playing for a win–but he violates another principle of winning chess: first equalize, then play for a win. By offering Black his choice of capturing (or not) he increases Black's winning chances and decreases his own. This is the fault of 18. Rb1?! an aggressive play when defense was better. Black could continue in a number of good ways–20... Nxb3 21. axb3 Rad8 and Black stands better is probably weakest. 20... Rad8 are all good. Why does Black not elect any of these plans? Failure to appreciate end-game advantages–Black is still playing the middlegame.

20... Bf5 21. Ra1 Nd3+ 22. Kf1 Rad8 23. Rd1 Bg4 24. h3 Bxf3 25. gxf3 Nc5 26. Ke2

White has made a battle of it. Black is committed to exchange his Knight for the superior Bishop producing a position still favorable for Black, but one that White should be able to draw. "The ending with Rooks," in the words of a chess wit, "is always drawn."

26... Nxb3 27. axb3 Kf8 28. e4 Ke7 29. f4 g6

The Category I player does not understand the endgame. If both Rooks are off the board

... a5 leads to a winning King and Pawn ending. Analyse. (Check *Basic Chess Endings* on the outside passed Pawn). Since Black would like to get both Rooks off the board to win, he should start by getting one Rook off. The Category I player may not win by 29... Rxd1 30. Rxd1 Rd8 31. Ra1 a6, but he will have made further progress toward the win.

30. Ke3 Ke6?!

Now Black cannot conquer the d-file without losing some tempi. White therefore equalizes.

31. h4 h5 32. Ra1 a6 33. Ra5!

This sudden activity of the White Rook is not accidental. The expert understands the Rook-less endgame is lost so he plans to activate his Rooks and this creates opportunities for himself. Black cannot prevent f5+ undoubling the White Pawns without disadvantage as 33... f5 34. e5 gives White ample play.

33... f6?!

Poor endgame play–Black allows his Pawns to become weakened. Plan a better defense for Black.

34. f5+ Kf7 35. fxg+ Kxg6 36. Rg1+ Kh6 37. Rf5

Diagram

By solid play White has overcome his inferiority of eight moves ago and now owns an advantage. Thus is the advantage frittered away because of the Category I player's lack of endgame technique (read: understanding). The next question the Candidate Master must ask himself is what winning plan can he adopt. Notice, too, that if Black had offered a draw eight moves ago, White would almost certainly have accepted. Now the draw offer is rejected. Timing of draw offers is also part of the Candidate Master's repertoire.

37... Rd6 38. c4

Looking to paralyze Black's Queenside by c5.

38... Re5 39. Kf4 Re8 40. f3 Rde6 41. Rg2

White could seize the d-file by Rd1, but he first temporizes expecting 41... R8e7 42. Rg8 with an easy win. Waiting for a mistake is OK, but 41. Ra1 and Ra5 immediately is slightly more efficient.

41... Rd8 42. Ra2 Rd3 43. R2a5 Rxb3 44. Rxh5+ Kg7 45. Ra1

This invasion of the Kingside will lead to a White win.

45... Kf8 46. Rg1 Ke7 47. Rg7+ Kd8

Naturally 47... Kd6 fails to 48. c5 mate.

48. Rh8+ Re8 49. R8h7

Driving the King further away to the Queenside, White wants to free his center Pawn.

49... Kc8 50. Rh6 a5!

139

Black seizes on his only chance, to push his own passed Pawn.

51. R6g6 a4 52. Rg8 Rxg8 53. Rxg8+ Kd7 54. Ra8 b5 55. h5

White has analysed out a winning position. The expert's advantage is calculating ability. Calculate a White win.

55... Rb1 56. h6 Rh1 57. h7 a3 58. h8(Q) Rxh8
59. Rxh8 b4 60. Ra8 Black Resigns

THE CARO-KANN DEFENSE

1. e4 c6 2. d4 d5 3. exd cxd 4. Bd3

This line, popularized by Fischer, has the advantage of unbalancing the Pawn position and moving into lesser known territory.

4... Nc6 5. c3 Qc7

Black prevents the Bishop from taking the f4-b8 diagonal. An immediate 5... e5 is also playable though White has play against the isolated d-Pawn.

6. Ne2 e6 7. Bf4 Bd6 8. Bxd6 Qxd6 9. Nd2 Nf6

Black knows that weaknesses should be avoided, but his game is tenable after 9... e5 and he will at least have some piece activity. The danger of remaining passive is his Bishop on c8. It is not enough to just develop pieces–Black should be making plans for his Queen Bishop, not just waiting for a chance to open up.

10. Ng3

White for his part should be planning to occupy e5 with 10. Nf3 0-0 11. Re1 and Ne5.

10... 0-0 11. Nf3 Bd7

"Development."

12. 0-0 Rab8 13. Re1 b5

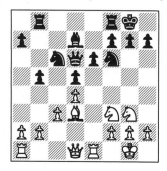

Battle lines have been joined. Black will play for Queenside action, White has center control and Kingside pressure: advantage to White. What plan should White follow?

14. a3?!

Deduct a few rating points if you selected this. Pawn moves on the side the opponent is attacking on are almost always errors. Since Black will play ... a5 and ... b4 the net result will be more open lines on the side Black has the advantage. The increased activity of the Rook on a1 is not compensation enough. Often this Rook will be exchanged leaving Black in greater control of the Queenside and White with one less attacking unit for his Kingside attack.

14... a5 15. Ne5 b4 16. axb axb 17. Ra6

Apparently strong, but this is still Black territory and should not lead to much. If Black plays carefully, White's misplaced play will rebound to Black's advantage. Still, White has a plan, and Black must play carefully to keep in the game. What is White's tactical plan?

17... bxc 18. bxc Qc7

Releasing the pin and beginning the siege of the c-Pawn.

19. Nxd7?!

White continues his Queenside action–the expert continues his plan of dominating the Queenside–stubborness can be a virtue! –but his Knight on g3 is poorly placed for any active center or Queenside play. The fact that Black's Pawn position is solid gives

Black the advantage. The only way White's plan can succeed is by tactical accident. The expert should know this, but just because Black has a slight edge now is no reason the Candidate Master should lose. The endgame is approaching and Black may find it very difficult to win such a position. So the Candidate Master keeps the pressure on, exchanging pieces, and waiting for his own chances to develop: good Swiss tournament-style play.

19... Qxd7 20. Qa4 Ne7

Releasing the pin–Black is defending well, not giving the Candidate Master an opening for superior tactical play.

21. Qa3 Rfc8 22. Ra7 Rc7 23. R1a1 Rxa7
24. Qxa7 Qxa7 25. Rxa7 Ng6

Though White maintains his superior Bishop, the ending remains solidly in Black's favor. Should White play for the draw with 26. Bxg6? Analyse.

26. Ne2

White refrains from exchanging his best minor piece. The doubled Pawns are not compensation enough. Keeping the Bishop also keeps alive White's (slim) hopes of turning around the game. Defending a game that has no real winning chances is much harder than defending a position that has counterchances.

26... Rb2 27. Ra8+ Nf8 28. f3 g6

Both sides defend against back-rank mates. What should White's plan be?

29. Kf1

Bringing the King to c1 to drive the well-placed Rook away and secure the Queenside. Once the King gets to c2, White should have little fear of losing.

29... Kg7 30. Ke1 N8d7 31. Ra7 h5?!

From this point on, Black begins to go astray. Black also cannot try for a win by 31... e5!? when White has to tread carefully–32. Kd1!? e4 33. fxe dxe 34. Bxe4 Nxe4 35. Rxd7 Rb1+ 36. Kc2 Re1 37. Nf4 winning (not 37. Kd3 Ne5+!)

32. Kd1 g5

Without a way to gain entry into White's Kingside, these Pawn moves constitute a weakening. Black is hardly lost but because he cannot find a solid endgame plan (in this case sitting still would be better) he begins to go astray and the Candidate Master's patience is rewarded.

33. Kc1 Rb8 34. f4!

Now both sides will end up with Pawn islands and the White Bishop will be more valuable than the Black Knight. Will this be enough to win? Not if Black finds the proper defense.

34... gxf?!

Once again Black avoids playing for ... e5. Better was 34... g4 35. f5 e5! when the fight is even. Black may be wondering why the Candidate Master is playing on in this "drawn" position. One fundamental fact of tournament warfare–the Candidate Master will fight for a win against a lower-rated player until there simply are no more chances left.

35. Nxf4 h4 36. Bc2 Kh6 37. Ba4

Diagram

37... Nb6?

Part of the will to win is also stamina. There are two kinds of stamina, physical and mental. Players with weak physical conditioning might consider a simple set of exercises: tournament play can be very exhausting. The better your physical conditioning, the less fatigue will effect your game. A tired body tires the mind.

Mental stamina frequently comes with the territory: the Candidate Master *knows* he is the superior player. He will wait patiently for his chances, believing that the Category I player will eventually crack and he will have his opportunity. How can one develop this mental stamina if one is weak there? Success is the best exercise. The more you win, the more you will win.

38. Rxf7 Nxa4 39. Rxf6+ Kg5 40. Rf7 Nxc3 41. Nxe6+ Kg6

White's patient and aggressive defense has led to a difficult endgame where White has all the winning chances. What are White's chances? How can he best utilize his extra Pawn?

42. Rf3 Rc8 43. Kd2 Ne4+ 44. Ke3 Rc3+ 45. Kf4 Rc2 46. Ke5

And a difficult win becomes much easier. Now mental stamina takes its further toll. Depression often sets in after a long struggle begins to go sour. The determination of the Category I player flags. The ending may be lost but he fails, as the Candidate Master did not, to put up the toughest defense. Defeat is envisioned and the vision produces reality. Best was 46... Nc3.

46... Kh5?! 47. Nf4+ Kh6 48. Nxd5 Ng5 49. Rf6+ Kg7
50. Kf5 Nf7 51. Rg6+ Kf8 52. Nf4

The difficult win becomes easy, and now it is only a matter of deciding which White Pawn will queen the easiest.

52... Rf2 53. Kg4 Rd2 54. Kxh4 Rxd4 55. Kg3 Ra4 56. Rf6 Kg7
57. Nh5+ Kg8 58. Rg6+ Kf8 59. h4 Ra3+ 60. Kh2 Ra4 61. g3

White needs only advance his Pawns carefully to win this position. An overzealous woodpusher might draw this position, but you are a Candidate Master. A little care and the two Pawns take on all the force of a Swiss avalanche.

61... Ne5 62. Rf6+ Ke7 63. Kh3 Ra5 64. Rf5 Kd6
65. Nf4 Ra1 66. Rf6+ Kd7 67. Re6

Candidate Masters who consider 67. Ng2 need to reevaluate their desire to play serious chess. Instead notice White's forceful play to dislodge Black's pieces from their aggressive post.

67... Nd3 68. Re2

Is the ending after 68... Nxf4+ any easier for Black? As long as the King is cut off from the Kingside, White will have no difficulties winning.

68... Rh1+ 69. Kg4 Nc5 70. h5 Nb7 71. Kg5 Nd8 72. Kg6 Rg1 73. Rg2 Re1 74. h6 Black Resigns

1. d4 d5 2. c4 c6 3. Nc3 Nf6 4. Nf3 Bg4

What does a Candidate Master do when he is faced with an apparent innovation in the opening? He should assume it is not as good as the normal line. This is a critical moment in the game. If the "innovating" side is allowed to get away with his innovation, he will have the advantage in the game. This innovation might even fool a Master. Analysis by GrandMaster Kotov gives 4... Bg4 a question mark as after 5. Ne5 Bf5 (the move that deserves the ?–5... dxc 6. Nxg4 Nxg4 7. e4 e5!? leads to very unclear complications) 6. cxd cxd 7. e4! Bondarevsky-Ovanesian, USSR 1947 lead to a quick win for White. What does this mean to the Candidate Master? One: OTB the Candidate Master must try to analyse the flaw behind Black's early divergence, and two: after the game he should review his opening play and not blindly believe what the books say. Chess is a fight, not just a memory contest, though knowledge *is* power.

5. cxd!?

Quite possibly stronger than Kotov's 5. Ne5. Black cannot respond 5... cxd. Why?

5... Bxf3

For his damaged Pawn position, White will obtain the two Bishops and support for his center.

6. gxf3 cxd 7. Qb3 Qd7 8. Bf4

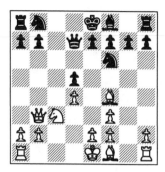

White has effectively taken charge of the position to this point. The problem with White's game is where to place his King. What plan should he take? Would 8. Bg5 have been better? Analyse.

8... Nc6 9. e3 e6 10. Rg1?!

White may feel that this is a non-committal move, restricting Black's King Bishop, but it effectively scotches White's Kingside castling. With the white-squared Bishop gone the weakness on g2 is not so significant. 10. Be2 Be7 11. 0-0 was a better line.

10... Nh5 11. Bg3 Bb4

With the two Bishops "recaptured" Black can afford to exchange his other Bishop for White's Knight keeping the position about equal.

12. Bd3 f5!?

Black is showing commendable aggression here. We have seen that Category I players are not bad attackers. Attack is usually easier to plan than defense. White needs to evaluate this position carefully, or he will find his game rapidly grow worse.

13. Be5!?

This is good play by the Candidate Master—he keeps the potential of his central mass alive. The battle is shifted to long-term planning.

13... Nxe5 14. dxe5 Bxc3+ 15. bxc3?!

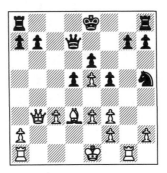

This further Pawn weakness will cause White many difficulties. Stronger was 15. Qxc3 0-0 (15... Rc8? Bb5!) 16. Ke2 Rfc8 17. Qd4 with good play (threat 17. Qh4, g6? Qxh5). White plans an eventual e4 opening up the center, but he is accumulating too many weak Pawns.

15... 0-0 16. f4!?

Although this prevents ... f4 by Black, it also locks up the Pawn position for some time. Notice the similarities between this game plan and the last game plan. Black's solid Pawn position means a direct attack will most likely fail. White therefore bides his time, waiting for Black to disturb his position significantly. This is not great chess, but it is usually quite successful against Category I players. The Candidate Master can try turning the board around at this point and planning a strong continuation for Black.

16... g6

Black solves one problem–how to get his Knight back in the game. He might visualize the plan ... Ng7-e8-c7-a8-b6-c4, but this is a rather tortuous journey. On g7 the Knight guards the square e6 which might be enough work out of this Knight for some time.

17. Rb1 Rab8

Not automatically responding ... b6 shows the Candidate Master that his opponent has some long-range grasp of the position.

18. Be2 Ng7 19. c4 Rfc8?!

More likely to be successful was 19... dxc followed by play on the c-file or d-file. Now both sides will have Pawn weaknesses. This increases the strength of the Bishop in this position. The Candidate Master takes a step toward victory.

20. cxd Qxd5 21. Qxd5 exd5 22. Kd2 Kf7 23. Rgc1

White begins to take over. By threatening 24. Rxb7+ he conquers the c-file.

23... b6 24. Ba6 Rxc1 25. Rxc1 Ne6 26. Rc8?

After 26. Rc6! White keeps his active Rook against Black's passive Rook and can improve the position of his King. Still, the expert's plan seems good, to play with the active Bishop against the Knight. Analyse.

26... Rxc8 27. Bxc8 Nc5

Now the Knight that seemed so paralyzed a few moves ago is solidly back in the game. The Queenside Pawn majority and the awkwardly placed White Bishop all add up to a plus and possible win for Black. The Candidate Master has to radically alter his thinking at this point in the game.

28. f3 Ke7 29. Kc3 Kd8 30. Bxf5 gxf5 31. Kd4 Ke7 32. Kxd5

The Candidate Master has tried to recover from his error, but the ending is lost. Should White resign? Find the Black win.

32... Na4?!

Black, a Category I player does not use his Knight effectively– the power of the Knight is that it can operate in more than one direction: 32... Na4 is single-directed (threat ... Nc3+). By 32... Nd3! (threat ... Nb4+ and ... Ne1 followed by ... Nxf3 and (eventually) ... Nxh2) Black uses his Knight like an expert. These small slips mark the difference between Category I and Candidate Master play. White is given a temporary reprieve.

33. Kc6 Nc3 34. a3 Nd1 35. e4

Eliminating another Pawn moves closer to the draw. Black's win slips further away with each Pawn exchanged.

35... fxe 36. fxe Ke6 37. Kb7 Nc3 38. Kxa7 Nxe4?!

Black's Pawn on b6 is doomed–he should then capture the a-Pawn and come back for the kingside Pawns with his Knight. The position may still be drawn, but he would keep his chances alive.

39. Kxb6 Nc3 40. Kc5 Nd5 41. Kd4 Nxf4

Black has killed the Pawn mass, but the a-Pawn will serve as a magnet to draw one of the two Black pieces across the board from the action. This means on the Kingside there will be equal material–and a draw. This is an example of lesser endgame understanding on the Category I player's part.

42. Ke4 Ng6 43. a4 Nxe5 44. Kf4

Heading for space on the Kingside–pushing the a-Pawn would also work, but White first takes his stand on the critical side of the board.

44... Nc6 45. Kg5 Kf7 46. Kh6 Kg8 47. Kg5

It would be an error to push the h-Pawn. Pushed too far it would take away maneuvering space for the White King and would eventually be lost when the draw, too, would disappear.

47... Kg7 48. Kh5 h6 49. Kg4 Kg6 50. Kh4 h5
51. Kg3 Kg5 52. Kh3 h4 53. Kg2 Kg4 54. Kf2 h3

Diagram

Black can't make progress after 54... Kh3 55. Kg1 Na5 56. Kh1 Nb3 57. Kg1 Kg5 58. Kg2

55. Ke3!

The Candidate Master must always be alert–55. Kg1 Kf3 56.

Kh1? Kf2 57. a5 Kf1 58. a6 Ne5 59. a7 Ng4 60. a8(Q) Nf2 mate. There is no reason to spoil many hours of play at the very end: mental stamina!

**55... Ne5 56. Kf2 Nc4 57. Ke2 Kf4 58. Kf2 Na5
59. Ke2 Kg4 60. Ke3 Nb3 DRAWN**

The Candidate Master defended dourly after his slip on move 26. The game also illustrates the importance of remembring there are two sides of the chessboard–the piece extra will dominate one side. By playing into the center (32... Nd3!) the Knight can leap to the undefended side, creating winning chances there.

1. d4 d5 2. c4 c6 3. Nc3 Nf6 4. Bg5 e6 5. e3 Be7 6. Bd3

You probably selected the more stereotyped 6. Nf3. The good of the dictum of Knights before Bishops holds here, too. Many players consider 6. Nf3 to be a fraction better, but chess is a game of fractions.

6... dxc 7. Bxc4 Nd5 8. Bxe7 Qxe7 9. Qb3?!

It is difficult to assign?! to this move–as the opening continues, White benefits from 9. Qb3. It does pressure the Queenside, develop a piece, and euchers Black into the following exchange, but the truth of the matter is that it is too early to commit the Queen. Better was 9. Nf3. The Queen may be needed on e2, c2, or even on the Kingside with Ne5 and Qg4-h5 depending on how the battle continues.

9... Qg5?!

Though Black forces White to forgo castling with 10. Kf1, the tempi lost are a greater advantage to White than the disadvantage of lost castling privileges.

10. Kf1 Nd7 11. Nf3

White spent nine minutes here analysing 11. Nf3, Qe7 12. e4 and the combinations arising from this sequence. He could have saved some valuable time by playing 11. Nf3 and thinking about

11... Qe7 12. e4 on his opponent's time. The Candidate Master knows he intends to play 11. Nf3 in the position. He knows, too, no other move (maybe 11. Ne4) needs serious consideration. By making the necessary move quickly, time may be gained on the clock.

11... Qe7 12. e4 N5b6 13. Bd3

Not so much to save the Bishop but following the time-honored dictum of Siegbert Tarrasch: avoid exchanges when your opponent's position is cramped.

13... 0-0

Black could gain an entirely different kind of game with 13... e5!? This is a different situation from the one that White faced on move 11: here Black had many options other than 13... 0-0. Castling was not a necessary move, only a tempting one.

14. e5!?

This is a very committing move–White announces his intentions of a Kingside attack, but his Queen is on the wrong side of the board, and he has to find a way to use his Rooks. This attacking play is easily combatted by a Master, but Black is not a Master.

14... h6

Better was ... c5 to begin to undermind the White center and seek the exchange of a few pieces (why?). Black reacts fearfully, but White was not threatening Bxh7+. By passive plays of this nature the Category I player allows the Candidate Master to bully him, to push him around on the chess board, and ultimately to defeat him.

15. Re1 Nd5 16. Bb1 f5?!

Black realizes now that ... h6 did not properly defend h7 (17. Qc2) and so plays to shut off the diagonal to his King. Notice how Black's response to a White threat (Bxh7+) was not part of a larger defensive plan, but an immediate move reaction. This is one point where the Candidate Master differs from the Category I player.

17. exf Qxf6

Diagram

Black's position suffers from some fundamental weaknesses: the Queen Rook and Bishop, the Pawn on e6, the long diagonal b1-h7. All of these added together would seem to indicate a quick win for White. Analyse a strong continuation.

18. h4?!

White could win material with 18. Qc2 (direct attack) as 18... Qf5 fails to 19. Qe2. To allow White to infiltrate by 19. Qh7+ Kf7 20. Ne4! would be decisive.

18... Rf7

Now Black can defend with ... Nf8 and has escaped immediate defeat, but the same problems remain.

19. Rh3 Nxc3 20. bxc3 e5

To prevent himself from choking to death, Black offers a Pawn. This is the penalty he now pays for his faulty plans on moves 9-16.

21. Qc2 Nf8 22. dxe Qe6

Diagram

A new stage of the game begins for the Candidate Master. He has a healthy Pawn plus and attacking chances. Should he expect the game to be over quickly?

23. Rg3 Qc4+ 24. Kg1 Bf5 25. Qd2?!

Endgames are difficult for the Candidate Master too: 25. Qb3!?

25... Bxb1 26. Rxb1 Qe6

By removing the light-squared Bishops, Black has eased his defensive tasks considerably (why?), but he remains down a Pawn. The Candidate Master needs to evolve a winning plan. The e-Pawn is obviously the key–if White can advance it, or the f-Pawn, a decisive Kingside attack becomes a reality.

27. Qe3?!

White offers the one concrete advantage, his extra Pawn, for the Kingside attack. Though this should still win, it is very untypical Candidate Master play. Because of the Pawn plus, there is no great hurry to initiate the Kingside attack. The Candidate Master is particular about his material–but he is willing to sacrifice material when he can *calculate* a greater gain. Here, 27. Qe3 has all the earmarks of a blunder rather than a sound sacrifice. Better was 27. Re1 to secure the e-Pawn. Then White threatens Nd4 with a deadly attack in the offing.

27... Qxa2 28. Re1 Kh8 29. h5

Though this blockades the weakened Kingside, White does better to free his f-Pawn by Nd4 and f4. Instead he plans to get his Rook on g3 to f4. It is now unlikely that White's attack will succeed. He is fighting with equal forces on the Kingside, White's King and f-and g-Pawns are unable to participate, for now, in the attack. Thus White's attack has been nipped. The even material means that Black's a-Pawn should become a counterforce in the game. Notice how the Candidate I player fails to use this counterchance, something the Candidate Master would never fail to do.

29... Re8 30. Rg4 Qe6 31. Rf4 Rxf4 32. Qxf4 c5

This keeps the Knight out of d4 but cedes the important d-file. White now has to win the game all over again. This time Black's King is unlikely to be able to participate in the defense. What does this mean in planning Black's defense: should he try to exchange Queens or not? Comment on the next four Black plays.

33. Qa4 a6 34. Rd1 b5 35. Qa5 Ra8 36. Rd6 Qc8 37. Nh4

Notice how Black, reacting defensively without a cohesive defensive plan, has been pushed steadily back. Now Black lashes out seeking counterplay. These nerve-reactions almost always backfire. Occasionally they succeed. The key is calculation. The Candidate Master has the ability to calculate a win against the scattered Black force.

37... Qg4?! 38. Ng6+ Kg8

Of course 38... Nxg6 39. hxg6 leaves Black in a permanent bind. You may have asked from the previous note, "How can the Candidate Master improve his ability to calculate?" One answer is to do it, and do it frequently. Calculate a win from this position. Frequent practice in calculation will produce a greater facility. Chess problems, such as mate in two or three, are not good exercise for tournament play–the positions are frequently ungame-like.

Mate in x-problems are their own reward. For practice in middle game analysis, analyse middle games. If you can find a player of similar strength, analysing with him can be especially beneficial.

39. Rd8 Rxd8 40. Qxd8 Qxh5 41. Qd5+!

Although taking the Knight at once would also win, the Candidate Master seeks the fastest way to win.

41... Kh7 42. Nxf8+ Kh8 43. Nd7 Qe8

There is no defense. White wins in a walk.

44. e6 c4 45. Qd6 Kg8 46. Ne5 a5 47. Qd7 Qb8
48. Qf7+ Kh7 49. Qg6+ Kg8 50. e7 Black Resigns

34

ALEKHINE'S DEFENSE

1. e4 Nf6 2. e5 Nd5 3. d4 d6 4. c4 Nb6 5. exd

White shows an unfamiliarity with this opening. The Candidate Master, who should be better prepared in the opening, should recognize this fact. How does the knowledge benefit Black. Psychologically it is not clear: different Candidate Masters will react in different ways. But chessically Black will find the conduct of this stage of the game easier to conduct. The advantage to the Category I player is that by avoiding the stronger but more complicated lines involved with 5. f4, he, too, will find the conduct of the game easier.

5... cxd

After 5... exd, the position becomes very equal. Black, for obvious reasons, chooses to keep the position complicated. This is proper play against a lower-rated player: complications favor the higher-rated player.

6. Nc3 g6 7. Be3 Bg7 8. Nf3 0-0 9. h3

White continues his campaign of avoiding complications in the opening. This is not good strategy in an unbalanced position (notice the Pawn structure). Switch Black's e-Pawn to c7 and h3 is harmless, perhaps even beneficial. With the unbalanced game, unless h3 fits into a plan of campaign, it is a waste of time.

9... Nc6 10. Be2 d5 11. c5

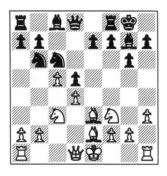

This is the hallmark of the Category I player's worst games: some strong moves, some weak moves. He fails, against the play of the Candidate Master, to find a unified plan in unfamiliar territory. The advantage of the first move keeps White's position sound, but he is courting disaster. This is the chess life in the battle between Category I and Candidate Master.

11... Nc4 12. Bxc4 dxc4 13. 0-0

What happens if White continues in an aggressive vein with 13. d5? Analyse. The Candidate Master should recognize the strength of the two Bishops in this unbalanced game. The exchange of a pair of Knights after 13. d5 Ne5 is part of the penalty of 9. h3

13... Bf5 14. Qd2 Bd3 15. Rfd1 Nxd4

Alexander Alekhine, who was perhaps for a very brief time a Category I player, said that in order to beat him, an opponent had to defeat him three times–once in the opening, again in the middle game, and finally in the endgame. This is resistance! The Candidate Master has scored overwhelmingly in the opening. Usually the Class A player will fold at this stage and a full point will be inked in on the wall chart. The Candidate Master must not score 1:0 on the score sheet just yet, however. He must play like a Candidate Master and finish off his opponent. What is Black's plan?

16. Nxd4 Bxd4 17. b4 Bg7?!

Diagram

Black wishes to preserve his two Bishops, but if he retreats in

this middle game, he is conceding that White's Bishop and Knight may be stronger. Compare White's Knight on c3 to the Bishop on d3. Now is the time to undermine White's only trump, the Pawn on c5. That occurs after 17... b6. If Black is more aggressively inclined, he can try 17... e5 followed by ... f5 and a Kingside attack based on the Pawn majority and more active Rooks; 17... Bg7 is not a Candidate Master move.

18. Rac1 Qd7

What is Black's plan? It has been said that a bad plan is better than no plan at all. Black has begun to drift. Waiting for an extra Pawn (e7) to suddenly queen is very poor chess.

19. Bh6 e5 20. Ne4

Black's lackadaisical play has allowed hope to develop in the White position. Suddenly d6 offers White play against c4 and the Pawn on c5 develops new strength. It is not too late for the Candidate Master to regroup, but waiting for your opponent to make a blunder is *hope chess* and usually does not work well. Opponents typically make errors when under pressure, not vacuum.

20... Qc6?! 21. Bxg7 Kxg7 22. Nd6 b5 23. a4 a6 24. Re1

Diagram

For the first time in the game White has a threat: Rxe5. This means that the Candidate Master has new problems to solve.

24... f6

Indicative of a mental attitude, Black continues to move on to defense. The reasoning is clear: he has a solid Pawn plus, but why should Black think defense? For the expert to feel he has to defend, a Pawn plus, a well-placed Bishop, a passed e-Pawn, does not augur well for the planning ability of the expert. Something is going sour. The Class A player who aspires to become a Candidate Master should take note of this attitude. Here is is the same attitude expressed by White's 5. exd and 9. h3.

25. f4!? e4

Black continues in his defensive mode shutting in his Bishop on d3 which, temporarily, takes on all the aspects of a large Pawn. Black's original advantage is thus diminished by his passive play from move 17 on. Some players, such as Grandmaster Tigran Petrosian, gained a reputation for passive play, but he was a GM, not a CM.

26. Qe3 bxa?!

The Candidate Master, admirably, still plays for a win–as he should do–but that hardest lesson for a Candidate Master to learn is when to stop playing for a win against a lower-rated player. Many an expert has exchanged an even position for a lost one by trying too hard. The opposite side of the coin is that many drawn or inferior positions have been won by such strategy. Overall, the Candidate Master will score more points by trying harder.

27. Nxc4 a3 28. Qd2 Rab8 29. Nb6
Diagram

Now that White's position is secure, a reevaluation is needed. Who has the advantage in this position?

29... Rfd8 30. Qa2

The battle has shifted. Unless Black can plan to use his e-Pawn, the war will slide over to advantage to White.

30... Rd4

Failing to rise to the occasion (not typical of a Candidate Master), the strain of fighting an opponent who resists proves too much. This is a lack of mental stamina. Black can preserve winning chances by 30... Rxb6! (Analyse.)

31. Qxa3 Qb5 32. Qa5!

Given the chance to be aggressive, the Class A player can play sound chess. The c-Pawn, established on move 11 as an error, becomes a terror. The Candidate Master is in difficulties–his King-side Pawn majority becomes meaningless.

32... Rxb4 33. Qxb5 Rxb5 34. Rc3 Kf7 35. Rec1

Diagram

White, given the opportunity to play to use his best Pawn, puts his full force behind it. Though down a Pawn, Black has severe problems if he cannot use his Bishop.

35... Ke6 36. g4 Rb2

Black passes an opportunity to confront White with a difficult endgame–Bishop and two Pawns vs. Rook. We have seen that the Class A player has difficulties defending such a position. 36...' R8xb6 would not lose for Black and may even win.

37. Nc4 Rb1

The Candidate Master is trying to regain control. If the Rooks are removed from the board, Black will win.

38. Nb6 Rxc1+ 39. Rxc1 g5?

This is the last move before time control–the ruiner of many games. What is the solution to time pressure? The answer to a large extent depends on the nature of the individual game. When presented with difficult problems move after move, sometimes time pressure is unavoidable. The reason that Black is in such difficulties, however, is his vacillating attitude in critical stages of the game. This is a harsh statement, but nevertheless true. It is better to expend almost all of one's time to evolve a comprehensive plan than to spend a little time responding to immediate threats.

40. f5+ Ke7 41. Nd5+ Kd7 42. c6+ Kd6 43. Nxf6 h6

Can White win the endgame? Can Black win the endgame? Analyse. View the endgame if all the pieces are removed.

Diagram

44. c7?! Rc8 45. Kf2 a5 DRAW

Evaluate this position. Should the Candidate Master have of-

fered the draw? This game illustrates that the endgame is the most difficult stage of the game for both the Candidate Master and the Candidate I player. The expert should strive to defeat his opponent in the middle game, but the Category I player cannot seek refuge in the endgame; to defeat a Candidate Master he must play better throughout the game.

35

THE QUEEN PAWN OPENING

1. d4 Nf6 2. e3

Class A players are attracted to systems like the Colle that are simple and energetic. The simplicity of the system (place a Bishop on d3, Pawn on c3, Knight on f3 to e5, Queen Knight to d2 and castle, advance e4 with a strong attack) is lulling. The Candidate Master should certainly try the Colle, but he needs to play more complex systems to improve his over-all grasp of the openings.

2... e6 3. Bd3 b6 4. f4 Ba6

The Candidate Master exactly pinpoints the flaws in White's order of moves. By exchanging white-squared Bishops, the main attacking unit of White's game is removed and White has the problem of his dark-squared Bishop. This happens because the Category I player is playing by rote.

5. Nf3 Bxd3 6. cxd3

With 6. Qxd3, White accepts his white-square weakness without any compensation and 6... d5 would then nail the e4 square.

6... d5 7. 0-0 Be7 8. Nc3 0-0 9. Ne5 N6d7

Black sails along. His plan is to extract White's attack by driving the White Knight off e5 or exchanging a piece or two against the endgame of White's Bishop on c1 versus Black's one e7.

10. e4 f6 11. Ng4

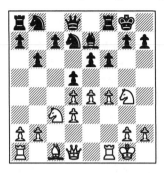

White, after allowing himself to be outplayed in the first few moves, has come back. He has kept his attacking chances alive. Now Black has a choice of playing 11... f5 to lock in the black-squared Bishop or 11... c5 to break open the center.

11... c5

Comment on this choice. Would the more defensive... f5 have been better?

12. exd cxd 13. Nb5 exd 14. Nxd4 Bc5 15. Be3

White has benefitted from the premature 11... c5. His better developed position has carried him to where the Class A player is back in the game.

15... Re8 16. Qf3 Nf8 17. Nf5

Black needs to consider how to survive the growing White attack. Analyse.

17... Nc6 18. Bxc5 bxc5 19. Rac1

Diagram

In this clearly favorable position, the Category I player offered a draw–should the Candidate Master take the draw offer?

19... Rc8

The decision to draw or not is always a tough one. Generally, it should be turned down unless Black will be forced into passivity,

decisive material loss, or complete winless chances. As this is not the case in this position, it is probably right to avoid the draw. The resulting position will be very difficult for the Candidate Master: his defensive abilities will be taxed. The old rule is that it is easier to win from a better endgame than an equal one; it is easier to win from an equal endgame than an inferior one; and it is easier to win from an inferior endgame than one in which you have already taken the draw. The Swiss system, in use in most U.S. tournaments, encourages this attitude. Whether or not it is healthy we will leave to the psychologists. Reality is sometimes its own answer.

20. Rxc5 Nd4 21. Qxd5+ Qxd5 22. Rxd5 Ne2+ 23. Kh1 Nxf4 24. Rd4 N8e6 25. Rd7 Rc7

Black must give ground here and exchange an active Rook. Black, of course, would like to use his pieces to plague White on the Queenside but after 25... Rc2 26. N5h6+ at least draws.

26. Rxc7 Nxc7 27. d4

Diagram

It might seem like madness that any Black player would spurn a draw for such a position. There is a lot of machsimo, chutzpah, confidence in chess. The Candidate Master still believes he will win or draw this position. He must believe thusly. If he believes he will lose this position, he will lose this position. Does this mean it was right or wrong to decline the draw on move 19? Think about it.

27... Re2 28. g3 Nfd5 29. Rc1

This Category I player plans to win this position–he plans 29... Rxb2 30. Ne7+ Nxe7 31. Rxc7 with invasion of Black's Queenside.

29... h5

Black is still looking for a win. The 3-Pawn vs. 2-Pawn advantage suggests the possibility of a Kingside attack. This is not wishful thinking; it is winning thinking. Even failing to gain an attack, Black will find development easier with chances to regain his material.

30. Nge3 g6 31. Nxd5 Nxd5 32. Rc5 Nb6 33. Nh4 Rxb2

Judging that now is the time to take the safe course, Black takes the b-Pawn. White can safely take on g6 now, and after 34. Nxg6 Rxa2 33. Rxh5, White would have winning chances. But the ending is still the most difficult part of the game. We can excuse the Category I player for missing this line. It only justifies Black's difficult choice on move 19.

34. Ra5 g5 35. Nf5 Rf2 36. Ne7+ Kf8 37. Rxa7

Diagram

White has captured the a-Pawn, but the Candidate Master can see the cost–scattered White pieces that don't function as a unit. A draw seems a likely outcome.

37... Rd2 38. Nc6 Nd5 39. Ra3 g4!?

Note that White's two Queenside Pawns are paralyzed while

Black uses his Pawn majority cleverly. This is the strength of the Candidate Master: using Pawn structures for his game plan.

40. h4?!

The last move of time control: White hopes to play Ra5 without having to worry about a back-rank mate.

40... gxh 41. Ra5 Nc3 42. Rxh5 Ne4

Now Black has established a number of threats against White's game. White is in serious difficulties.

43. Rh8+ Kg7 44. Rh4 Nf2+?

Sometimes, as in the tale of the purloined letter, what is most obvious escapes us. Why would a Candidate Master overlook mate in two? Time limit is of no concern – that was on move 40. Such things happen. The Candidate Master must learn to control these errors. Part of the problem is that from move 19 on, Black has been trying to improve the position of his pieces. Apparently he wants to bring his f-Pawn into the fray and thus avoids 44... Nxg3+ 45. Kg1 Rg2 mate. Blunders like this spoil the esthetic appreciation of the game but don't diminish the fighting knowledge the student can gain.

45. Kh2 f5 46. a4?

White, too, is blind. This phenomena of double blindness appears very frequently in chess. One side makes a blunder and the other side believes in it. White is depressed, harried for so long by the Black forces. Without thinking very long about 46. Rxh3!?,

White continues.

46... Ng4+ 47. Kxh3 Rh2 mate

1. e4 c5 2. c3 d5 3. Bb5+

White usually does not make this check first. Normal is to exchange center Pawns with 3. exd.

3... Bd7 4. Qa4?!

White should first exchange Bishops by 4. Bxd7+ when 4... Nxd7 is not so good for Black (5. exd and White is OK) so 4... Qxd7 5. exd with even play.

4... dxe 5. Bxd7+ Qxd7 6. Qxe4 Nf6 7. Qe3 e6

Black has clearly won the battle of the opening. What plans can he make to further increase his advantage?

8. Nf3 Nc6

Black continues to pressure d4. The weakness on the d-file will lead to a strong Black initiative. White will find his Bishop on c 1 a handicap especially with d3 as weak as it is. Black has a very strong game.

9. Na3 Nd5 10. Qe2 Nf4 11. Qe4

White is willing to throw a Pawn to Black's jaws. Perhaps he reasons he can catch a stuffed knight, but there is no reason to believe that White can outcombine Black from an inferior position. With development quantitatively equal but qualitatively in Black's favor, Black knows that general principles tell him he can capture the g-Pawn. All the Candidate Master needs to do is calculate the method.

11... Nxg2+ 12. Kf1 f5 13. Qa4

Painful would be 13. Qc4 Na5! 14. Qb5 Nf4 15. Qxa5 Qd3+

13... b5!

Retaining the piece by returning the Pawn. Black has played in true Candidate Master style, increasing his opening advantage. White, in Category I style, fails to evolve a long term plan, responding to each Black move rather than trying to establish a plan.

14. Nxb5 Nf4 15. Qxf4 Qd3+ 16. Ke1?! Qxb5

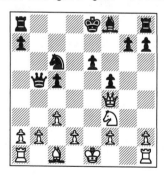

White first identified the problem of his Bishop on c 1 as early as move 8. Since that time he has failed to solve the problem of the Bishop and, by extension, the Queen Rook.

17. Qc7

A word should be said for White's active play: it will defeat many lesser-rated players. The Candidate Master beats the Category I player by using superior strategy. Notice that Black could still err here by 17... Rd8 18. Ng5 Rd7 19. Nxe6! and it would be the Class A player who would be showing the game and telling how he "outplayed" the Expert.

17... Qb6! 18. Qxb6 axb6

The ending favors Black. He has two Pawn "islands" compared to White's three (soon to be more!). His Rook on a8 suddenly "develops" and his bishop on f8 has potential to be a very good Bishop. White's position, on the other hand, still has the dilemma of the Bishop on c1 and the d-Pawn will be weak. Is the game lost for White?

19. d4?!

Whether White was lost on the previous move is a question for annotators and theoreticians. For the OTB player the question is "How can I best improve my game?" The Candidate Master recognizes this, constantly looking for ways to improve his piece position and Pawn formation. A Candidate Master would settle upon 19. d3 for his choice of moves, when after 19... Bd6 20. Be3 Ke7 the battle would still be on.

19... cxd 20. Nxd4 Nxd4 21. cxd4 Bd6

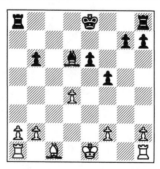

The nature of the endgame has changed. White now has the

problem of a semi-bad Bishop on c1, but three isolated Pawn islands. Black also has a lead in development, a factor as important in the endgame as it is in the middle game or opening. Turn the board around–what long range plan could you suggest for White's survival?

22. h4 O-O 23. f4?!

If you decided White's best chance for survival was to use his Queenside majority, you are thinking like a Candidate Master. By 22. Be3 (idea of d5 and Bxb6 relieving himself of the isolated d-Pawn), b5 23. a3 O-O 24. O-O-O!? Now White's Bishop on c1 has erected a barrier, not against Black's Kingside Pawn majority, but against itself.

23... Rfc8 24. Rh2?

In a natural desire to prevent an invasion on c2, the Category I player blunders away a few Pawns. This was to be expected watching the conduct of the game over the last few moves.

24... Rxc1+ 25. Rxc1 Bxf4 26. Rhc2 Bxc1 27. Rxc1 Rxa2 28. Rc6 Rxb2 29. Rxe6 Kf7

Black has cleverly simplified into a winning ending. The Candidate Master knows the best thing to do with a winning ending is to win it. He does not prolong the game needlessly, but seeks the quickest way to convince the Category I player to resign.

30. Re3 Rb4 31. d5 Rd4 32. Re5 Re4+ White Resigns

1. d4 Nf6 2. c4 d6 3. Nc3 g6 4. e4 Bg7
5. Nf3 0-0 6. Be2 N8d7 7. 0-0 e5 8. dxe

The Candidate Master may wonder how to improve his end-game technique. There are two sound methods: study endgame works–there are a number of good books on the subject and many chess magazines, notably *Chess Life*, that have endgame columns. The second method is for the Candidate Master to deliberately play for the endgame in his tournament or postal games. This can give extra confidence to the Candidate Master who will benefit by experience. The key to this second method is to analyse the end-game afterwards and learn both from his own mistakes and his opponent's.

8... Nxe5 9. Nxe5 dxe5 10. Qxd8 Rxd8 11. Bg5 c6 12. Rad1 Rxd1

Black begins to slip–he feels he cannot hold the d-file by 12... Be6 13. Rxd8 Rxd8 14. f4 when Black has some problems, failing to notice that 14... Re8 15. fxe Nd7 when Black has good play. The Candidate Master thus gains a small but real advantage: the open, uncontested d-file.

13. Rxd1 Be6 14. f3

Opening up an entrance to the center for his King. A note about this ending: This is a difficult ending to win. Why? Analyse.

14... Nd7?!

Black, too, has a problem in this ending. White has only minimal winning chances because of the balanced Pawn position, but Black has to find squares for his pieces. If he simply sits, White will continually improve his game until he can engineer a breakthrough. Plan?

15. Nd5!?

This contains the disturbing threat of Nc7 which is quite difficult to meet. Thus the Candidate Master gains further inroads against his opponent.

15... cxd5 16. cxd5 Bxd5 17. Rxd5!?

White could, and should, try 17. exd5!? With the two Bishops and a passed d-Pawn, he will have achieved the unbalanced Pawn position he needs. The text keeps the two Bishop advantage, but with the Pawn position still balanced as the edge of the Bishops is only slight. Still, White has made further advances.

17... Nf8 18. Be3

With Black's pieces huddled far away from the Queenside, White focuses his Bishops there. Black is in trouble. White is playing a steady, aggressive endgame. This is a combination the Category I player will find hard to combat.

18... Ne6 19. Rd7 Nd8

Diagram

This position is one that faces the handler of the 2B's often. Should he win a Pawn and play with opposite colored Bishops or further strive to strengthen his position. Analyse.

20. Bxa7

White goes for the immediate gain of a Pawn, but 20. Bc4 Bf6 21. Bd5 will win a Pawn (or more) without giving Black the choice of Bishops of opposite colors. As a general rule, the holder of the Two should not stop to pocket a Pawn by allowing opposite colored Bishops unless he can calculate a win or can find no way to increase his advantage. The Candidate Master needs to be willing to learn to play opposite colored Bishop endings also, though. Suffice it to say that the Pawn plus is a Pawn plus,and the ending takes on a different hue.

20... Rxa7 21. Rxd8+ Bf8 22. Bc4

First 22. Rd7 fails to 22... Rxa2 23. Bc4 Rxb2! 24. Rxf7 Bc5+ 25. Kf1 b5! 26. Bd5 Bd4 with increased drawing chances as the Queenside Pawns disappear.

22... b6 23. Rb8 Kg7 24. Kf1 Bc5 25. Ke2 Ra4 26. Kd3 Ra7

Diagram

White has made progress. What is the next step in his plan?

27. a3

White obviously has to advance his Queenside Pawns. Is 27. a3 an efficient way to begin?

27... Bd4 28. Kc2 h5

Black seeks counterplay on the Kingside. This is the proper decision for the Category I player. If he does nothing, the Candidate Master will gain a passed Pawn on the Queenside and win decisive material. Only by playing on the Kingside can Black prevent loss.

29. Kb3 Kh6 30. a4 Kg5 31. Rf8 f5
32. exf gxf 33. Bd3 f4 34. Rg8+ Kh4?!

Black enters into very dangerous waters. White can paralyze the Black forces after 35. Bf5! Bf2 36. Rg6! Rf7 37. Be6 Rc7 38. Kb4 with a winning position. Endgames are difficult for all players. The Candidate Master should study these endings. They occur frequently between fairly evenly matched players.

35. g3+? Kh3 36. gxf exf 37. Rg5 Ra5 38. Bf1+ Kxh2 39. Rg8

The slip on move 35 has allowed Black into the game, but here is where mental stamina comes into play. The Candidate Master still has his Queenside Pawns, and, also important, the Category I player will find the kaleidoscopic shift in the game hard to assimilate. In other words, the Category I player's greatest danger here is that he may be distracted from 40 moves of solid defense and go off on some quixotic plan. As a Candidate Master, analyse carefully what Black should do.

39... Re5 40. Bc4 Re3+ 41. Kb4 Rxf3
42. Be2 Rg3 43. Rd8 Bxb2 44. Bxh5 f3?!

With plenty of time left on his clock (second time control) Black makes an elementary blunder. This occurs because of the relief of not having to defend produces a lessening of concentration. It is this lack of concentration–of planning a winning or drawing game (the "anything wins/draws attitude" that afflicts the Category I player–that justifies the Candidate Master into playing out "hopelessly drawn" endgames. It is not Grandmaster chess, it is down-home Swiss system chess and it is often points on the wall chart.

45. Bxf3 Rxf3 46. Rd2+ Kg3 47. Rxb2 Rf5

The Category I player who has probably not studied R+P endings does not know the importance of getting his King back to the Queenside–even at the cost of his b-Pawn.

48. Re2

Whereas the Candidate Master knows he must cut off the

Black King.

48... Ra5 49. Re6 Ra6

Black's Rook has been reduced to passivity–a very bad sign in Rook and Pawn endings. The Candidate Master knows it is better to discard the b-Pawn to activate his Rook.

50. Kb5 Ra5+ 51. Kb4 Ra6 52. Rd6

White, too, flounders. What is a winning try for White?

52... Kf4 53. Rd4+ Ke5 54. Rh4 Kd6 55. Kb5 Ra8 56. Kxb6

At last–and at the cost of a few tempi–White has captured the hated b-Pawn to reach a book draw. But tournament players are not allowed to consult books during play. As a Candidate Master you should know the drawing technique–*well*. If you do not, halt the study, get an endgame book, and study this ending now. Then return to the game position and criticize Black's defense.

56... Rb8+ 57. Ka7 Rb2 58. a5 Kc7 59. Rc4+ Kd7 60. Rg4 Kc7 61. Rg7+ Kc8 62. a6 Rb3 63. Rb7 Rh3 64. Rb4

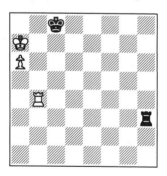

What is Black's best play?

64... Rh7+

Is this playable? Analyse.

65. Ka8 Rh6?

This loses. Can Black save the game by 65... Rc7? What about 65... Rh1? What about 65... Rg7? Study this critical position.

66. Rc4+ Kd7 67. Kb7 Black Resigns

A game that illustrates that 64 adequate moves can be negated by the lack of study of a fundamental endgame.

1. d4 Nf6 2. c4 c5 3. Nf3

The Candidate Master needs to decide on the opening that best suits his tyle. Here he had a choice of the aggressive Benoni with 3. d5, but he may not like the Benko Counter Gambit. These are decisions that are best made not OTB but at home or by correspondence. Here the Candidate Master elects a quieter system.

3... cxd 4. Nxd4 e5

But Black insists on playing a complicated system. The Candidate Master should not decide because he elected to play a "quiet" system that he should play passively. He should proceed on "faith"–White has made no weak moves: there is no reason why on move five he should retreat.

5. Nb5 d5 6. cxd Bc5

The Category I player is more than capable of seeing that 6... Nxd5? is a piece-losing blunder.

7. e3

But this is unnecessarily passive. The same logic that led White to 5. Nb5–White has made no weak moves–should lead the CM to decide on a choice of White moves: 7. N1c3, 7. N5c3 or 7. d6. Each has its own advantages. Which would you select? (No credit for 7. Bg5?)

7... O-O 8. N5c3 e4 9. Be2

Immediate pressure on e4 by 9. Nd2 Re8 10. Bb5 Re5!? has its adherents, notably Russian theorist Gipslis. White's plan of preparing for castling is solid, sound play: good strategy against an aggressive Class A player. Black must prove the soundness of his Pawn sacrifice. A master might demonstrate the soundness of Black's game. The Class A player will find this most difficult against play that does not leave weaknesses in its trail.

9... Re8 10. N1d2 Nxd5?

The Category I player does not follow the details of the position. Black's strong point is e4 which is under pressure. Nimzovich in *My System* prescribed overprotection. 10... Bf5 keeps the e4 square safe and the d5 Pawn under attack. After 10. O-O Na6, Black can use all his pieces to conquer d5–this is Candidate Master planning. The Class A player fails to find this idea.

11. N2xe4 Nxc3 12. Qxd8 Rxd8 13. Nxc3

And an endgame has been reached. The Candidate Master, you, is a full Pawn ahead. What is the simplest winning plan?

13... Nc6 14. Bd2

This is not the simplest plan–14. e4 shuts off the f5 Bishop's diagonal but opens up the c5 Bishop and d4 for the Knight. Best is 14. O-O. White has a safe King and no weaknesses. This can be followed up by, say, 14... Nb4 15. Ne4 Bg6 16. Bd2 Nc2 17. Rad1 with an advantageous endgame.

14... Bf5 15. 0-0-0?!

White is courting danger here–Black should respond 15... Nb4 as 16. Be1 is met by 16... Rac8 (threatening 17... Nxa2+! 18. Nxa2 Bxe3 mate) with counterplay. White's error is in the seriousness of the counterplay he allows. After 15. 0-0, if Black should somehow break through on the Queenside, he may regain his Pawn. After 15. 0-0-0, if Black somehow breaks through on the Queenside, he may win a King.

15... Ne5?!

Typical Class A play–Black properly focuses on d3 but Nb4 attacks both d3 and a2 (mate!?). Pieces function much better when they attack two important squares. Sometimes the opponent gets confused! Not great art but practical chess.

16. e4

A dual-purpose move shutting out Black's white-squared Bishop and protecting d3.

16... Be6 17. Bf4 Ng6

Black is in retreat.

18. Rxd8+

A Master would play 18. Bg3 first. Why? (As a potential Candidate Master you must realize that upon attaining your goal of a 2000-2199 rating, you will eventually want to understand master play).

18... Rxd8 19. Bg3 f5 20. exf Bxf5 21. Rd1 Rc8 22. Bf3 Ba3?!

Black sees that 22... b5 fails to 23. Bb7 so he tries his best to disrupt White's position, but notice how the Candidate Master evaluates the position. He notes that White's real advantage lies on the Kingside (3 P's vs. 2). With minor pieces being even, the Candidate Master defends by 22... b6!? and there will be a long, hard struggle for White to realize his advantage. The difficulty behind 22... Ba3 is that it will cede the two Bishops with an unbalanced (Pawn +) Pawn position. Once again the Category I player tries to solve his problems move by move rather than looking at the board as a whole.

23. bxa3! Rxc3+ 24. Kb2 Rc2+ 25. Kb3

Black has "conquered" the seventh rank, doubled White's a-Pawn–but to what advantage? None. White has a winning position. The Candidate Master who has studied 2B's vs. N+B will know how to proceed.

25... Rc5 26. Rd2

The Rook is well-placed here, freeing the g3 Bishop and preventing a possible disruptive Bc2+

26... Be6+ 27. Kb2 Rb5+ 28. Kc1 Bf5 29. Kd1 b6?!30. Bd5+

The end now comes suddenly if you can describe 30 moves of outplaying one's opponent sudden. Quickly analyse why 30... Kf8 loses.

30... Kh8 31. Bb3! h6 32. Rd8+ Kh7 33. Bg8+ Black Resigns.

A game that illustrates both the strengths and weaknesses of the Candidate Master.

1. d4 Nf6 2. Nf3 c5 3. e3 d5 4. c3 Nc6 5. Bd3

The Colle System has been an attractive opening to the rank and file chess player for about fifty years. The attraction, of course, is the attacking possibilities it offers; the simplicity of the plan: Bd3, 0-0, N1d2, Re1, and e4; and the fact that since Grandmasters no longer play this line too often, it is relatively unstudied by lesser players.

The drawback is that a knowledgeable opponent can equalize too easily. Are you, as a Candidate Master, knowledgeable? White's setup is easily understood. What is Black's? There are a number of anti-Colle systems. A study of how to conduct the Black side of this opening will be beneficial to the Candidate Master.

5... Bg4

Specialized books on the opening, in this case such as Koltanowski's *Colle System*, can also be beneficial–especially if the Candidate Master plans to play a particular opening frequently. Here we can discover Black's plan of exchanging the Queen Bishop for White's King Knight, weakening White's grip on e5.

6. N1d2

White would jump into Black's scheme by playing 6. h3 Bxf3 7. Qxf3 c4 8. Bc2 e5 9. dxe Nxe5 10. Qe2 Be7 with equality according to Sokolov. Is this position one you would like to play as

Black?! If not, you need to find another system to play against the Colle.

6... e6

A Candidate Master who knows the point (weaken e5) behind... Bg4 would not hesitate to throw his Category I opponent into a fret by 6... e5!? Such a move, aside from being good chess, is also good psychology. The Category I player is a poor defender–6... e5 will make it appear that he has lost the opening advantage–and he has. This was Black's easiest shot for equality (or the advantage). Now White comes back into the game.

7. Qa4

Another thematic idea in the Colle–White breaks the pin and threatens Ne5. The Candidate Master has to find a way to diminish the pressure on both e5 and c6. What is the thematic defense? What is Black's plan?

7... Nd7 8. 0-0

White should continue pressure with 8. Bb5 Qc7 (Black continues to reinforce both c6 and e5 and is well on his way to equality) 9. dxc Bxf3 10. Nxf3 Nxc5 and Black has equal play. What plan should Black now follow for the placement of his pieces?

8... Nb6

This sidetracks the Knight. Black would have better chances if he concentrated on e5–avoiding only the trap 8... Qc7 9. Re1 Bd6? (9... Be7) 10. dxc winning.

9. Qc2 Rc8 10. dxc Bxc5 11. e4

Diagram

Though Black has a lead in development, since his King is uncastled and his Knight on b6 is misplaced, he cannot benefit from the opening up of lines. The Candidate Master therefore seeks to keep lines closed. This falls into the preset White plan of attack, however. An alternative might be 11... dxe 12. Nxe4 Be7 when White has only a small edge. As a practical try, Black's next is

OK. It keeps the position closed and complicated, but it does not resolve his two main problems–the uncastled Black King and White's growing initiative.

11... d4 12. Bb5

But the Category I player moves away from the expected. The Candidate Master knows the general outline of White's attacking plan–Re1 e5 Ne4 etc. *When the opponent makes a move clearly not part of the expected plan, careful scrutiny of the position is needed.* This careful checking will produce a plan to "bust" the opponent's game or avoid being busted in return by some surprise tactics.

12... 0-0 13. Bxc6 Bxf3

If he had analysed carefully before the "natural" move 12... 0-0 he would have forseen the difficulties heading his way and have found the *zwischenzug* 13... d3! when he would keep the position alive. Black's problem here is that he failed to recognize a critical point and is allowing his opponent to outplay him tactically.

14. Nxf3 Rxc6 15. Rd1

Diagram

Black by now will recognize he has been outplayed. Apparently he cannot try 15... Rd6 16. b4 d3 17. Qb3 d2 as 18. Bb2 wins a piece. There is a flaw in this analysis however. What is it?

15... e5?!

Black has grown discouraged–he believes he is lost and so creates a losing position. Depression of this kind is very difficult to overcome. A certain stubbornness of mind is the mark of the master. A master would find 15... Rd6 16. b4 dxc! when Black is still in the fight. The Class A player who desires to become a Candidate Master must try to develop that same mental toughness.

**16. Nxe5 Re6 17. cxd Bxd4 18. Nf3 Rd6
19. Nxd4 Rxd4 20. Be3 Rxd1+ 21. Rxd1 Qf6**

Black has no compensation for the Pawn minus. A long, painful struggle seems to be in store for the Candidate Master.

22. Bd4 Qe6 DRAWN

The Candidate Master offered the draw here–no harm in that–and the Class A player accepted. Once again the Class A player who expects to progress must learn to beat–or at least try to beat–his expert opponent. After 23. b3 Rc8 24. Qd3 Rd8 25. f3 White would have good winning chances. Though the Category I player might not win, and, as we have seen, might even lose, he would learn more about chess and more about his own abilities to continue the fight. Taking the draw in such positions is a good way to remain a Category I player.

1. e4 c5 2. c3 Nc6 3. d4 cxd 4. cxd d5 5. exd Qxd5 6. Nf3 Bg4

This move is playable but not as good as 6... e5 7. Nc3 Bb4 8. Bd2 Bxc3 9. Bxc3 e4! was shown to be equal in Nimzovich-Chajes. The Category I player may have residual memories of the Nimzovich Defense which this position resembles–1. e4 Nc6 2. d4 d5 3. exd Qxd5 4. Nf3 Bg4 when 5. Be2 is best as 5. Nc3 Bxf3! 6. Nxd5 Bxd1 7. Nxc7+ Kd7 8. Nxa8 Bg4 leads to Black's advantage. This is one of the dangers of relying on memory: memories are often inexact.

7. Nc3!

The Candidate Master who plays an off-beat opening like the Alapin Variation should be well-prepared. The move that is weak against the Nimzovich is strong in the Alapin Sicilian. What is the difference?

7... Qd8?!

Black avoids 7... Bxf3 8. gxf3 Qxd4 9. Qxd4 Nxd4 10. Nb5! and Black gets the inferior position. This is the kind of position that the Candidate Master needs to spend the proverbial midnight oil on. Besides consulting the books, the Candidate Master may decide the evaluation of this position is wrong. Such a study (instead of memorization) is very valuable to the Candidate Master. He will learn typical middle-game and endgame patterns of this line. If the player aspiring to Candidate Master rating has a chess computer, feeding this line into it and playing out the various lines can aid him also. Five minute chess, with an eye to the different chances for Black and White should be noted.

A thorough knowledge of a line like the Alapin can be of great value for practical tournament play. Here the Candidate Master's opponent errs badly and the game quickly takes on the appearance of a rout. How can White crush Black?

8. d5 Nb8

Black sees that 8... Ne5 loses a piece by what?

9. Qa4+

Driving Black back even more as 9... Qd7 loses to 10. Bb5.

9... Bd7 10. Qb3 Qb6?!

Understandably Black tries to limit White's attacking chances but this move cedes a Pawn with no relief afterwards. The position hardly appears defensible after 10... Qc8 11. Bf4 Nf6 12. Rc1 so he heads for a lost endgame. It is better for the Category I player to go into an endgame loss than a middle game loss. Technique is still difficult for the Candidate Master, but it is still stretching things to imagine that the endgame has been reached just because only the Queens disapper.

11. Qxb6 axb6 12. Be3 Nf6 13. Bxb6

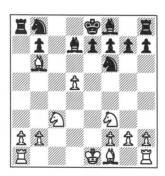

White has stolen a Pawn with a winning game–or so the annotators would say. But the annotators don't have to sweat through the hard pressure of the tournament game. Some players have a tendency to play very strongly until they establish a winning position, and then they relax. White's winning position amounts only to the Pawn on a2–and that is still a long way from becoming an active participant in the game.

Many a boxer has gotten up, after being knocked to the canvas, to come back to win. Eternal vigilance is the price of victory.

13... e6

By destroying the strong White Pawn on d5, Black will be able to develop his pieces, but the danger is that the White lead in development may flair up again. Analyse the alternative 13... g6. White keeps the initiative by 14. Bc4 Bg7 15. 0-0 0-0 16. Rfe1 with the advantage. So, practically, 13... e6 is better.

14. dxe Bxe6 15. Nd4 Bd7 16. Ndb5 Bxb5?!

The Category I player has found defense to be very difficult and so swaps pieces, but this allows White's lead in development to expand from 3 to 2 (1.5x) to 3 to 1 (3x)–nearly decisive as the center is wide open. Though Black's position is shaky and probably lost, stouter defense can be had by 16... Na6 17. 0-0-0 Be7 18. Re1 Kf8!? with some small chance for survival. Now White's two Bishops should prove decisive. Analyse White's chances.

17. Bxb5+ N8d7 18. 0-0?!

There are some chess players who thrive on the challenge. They can play well, usually establishing an advantage even against higher-rated players. Then the advantage dissipates and the challenge begins all over again. The loss of advantage occurs because of the attitude "any move wins in this position." The Candidate Master should know that chess is not only a struggle, it is also an art. The Candidate Master should strive for elegance, for chess is an elegant game. It is more than aesthetics–the efficient victory allows the Swiss player a chance to rest before his next round. When the game is unnecessarily prolonged–sometimes for hours–the toll is often taken in the next round. After 18. 0-0-0 Black will find it impossible to survive without losing at least a piece. (Analyse and confirm).

18... Be7 19. Rad1

Find a last-chance defense for Black

19... Bd8!? 20. Bxd7+ Nxd7 21. Rfe1+ Kf8 22. Bxd8?!

White continues in his lackadaisical approach to winning his won game. In the spirit of "anything wins" he selects a simple line that allows Black to prolong the struggle. With 22. Rxd7 Bxb6 23. R1e7 Bd4 24. Rxf7+ Kg8 25. g3 and Black will not survive.

22... Rxd8 23. Na4?!

White has been content with his sloppy play. The practical player may ask why not? White still has a winning game. But had White played 18. 0-0-0 the game would be over. And witness what is to come. Analyse for yourself the best way to break Black's position.

23... Re8!

Black has been resourceful in the last few moves. The Category I player can often find the *only* move in a difficult position. It is when he is faced with a choice that the difficulties arise. This escape clause is why White should have found 23. Re3! g6 24. h3 (emphasizing Black's helplessness) h5 25. R3d3 Ke7 26. Nd5+ Ke6 27. Nb6 winning. Of course White can omit 24. h3 h5.

24. Kf1 Rxe1+ 25. Rxe1 f6

The win that was easy seven moves ago becomes considerably more difficult. The Candidate Master should learn from these slips, but now an entirely different problem faces the Candidate Master. How does he win this position? Can he win this position? What plan should White follow?

26. Nc3?

This game illustrates a truth that may hurt–Candidate Masters can be guilty of some terribly weak play. Although usually consistently strong, experts *are* sometimes inconsistent. The jump from Class A to expert is not a long journey. Practice, study, desire, and effort to find the best move in any position will carry you far. What is the winning line our expert missed in this game? Analyse.

With a little study you should have found 26. Rc1 Ke7 27. Rc7 with a second Pawn or a winning King and Pawn endgame. Alertness!

26... Kf7 27. Nd5 Ne5

Is the endgame after 27... Re8 28. Rxe8 Kxe8 easier or tougher for Black? What are your thoughts on the matter?

In general, endgames should be judged on the King and Pawn position. Since White wins if the Rooks and Knights are exchanged, each step toward that King and Pawn endgame favors the materially-better off position. The endgame after 27... Re8 would be tougher for Black.

28. f4 Nc6 29. Rd1

This rather mysterious Rook move eventually proves to be Black's undoing. Black will see that White wants to invade on d7 with his Rook. After 29... Ra8 30. a3 Ra4 (active Rook!) 31. g3 b5! the invasion of d7 lacks the kick of attacking b7. The ending may still be lost for Black, but he is fighting.

29... Rd8?!

This move is fundamentally bad because as we have seen, the exchange of Rooks favors White. The pin is a non-pin because Nc3 breaks the pin immediately with either an invasion on d7 or the exchange of Rooks.

30. Ke2 Ke6 31. Nc7+ Kf5 32. Rxd8 Nxd8

A new stage of the endgame has been reached. As we have seen, the Knight endgame is more easily won than the previously discussed endgame. How does the Candidate Master know this? Besides the theoretical background we have discussed, confidence grows from knowledge: by studying the technique of endgame virtuosos (Lasker, Rubinstein, Capablanca, Fischer, etc.) the Candidate Master knows that he can enter certain endgames confident that a win is available. This allows him to select simplifying lines he might otherwise avoid out of doubt.

33. Kf3 h5 34. g3

Even Class B players know that 34. h3? is an error here.

34... g5 35. Nd5 Nc6

Locking the Pawn position by 35... g4+ only frees White to move to the Queenside. Black needs to exchange off Pawns, not lock them. Why?

**36. Ne3+ Ke6 37. fxg fxg 38. Ke4 Ne5
39. h3 g4 40. hxg hxg 41. Kd4**

White, of course, heads to the side of the board he is stronger on. Black cannot contest the invasion by 41... Kd6 as 42. Nc4+ completes the theoretical transformation to a King and Pawn endgame win.

41... b5 42. b4! Kd6

Now the Candidate Master in White wakes up and creates a neat combination to win the b-Pawn. This should be worked out to the end. Work it out.

**43. Nf5+ Ke6 44. Ng7+ Kd6 45. Ne8+ Ke6
46. Nc7+ Kf5 47. Nxb5 Nf3+ 48. Kd5 Nd2**

Black could resign at this stage. The Candidate Master has the win in hand–finally!

**49. Nd4+ Kg5 50. b5 Nf1 51. b6 Nxg3 52. b7 Nf5
53. Nxf5 Kxf5 54. b8(Q) Kg5 55. Ke4 Black Resigns**

An endgame that the aspiring Candidate Master can learn much from.

1. e4 e5 2. Nf3 Nc6 3. Bb5 a6 4. Bxc6

Because of a famous game, Lasker-Capablanca, St. Petersburg 1914, and the view of the annotator, this line has been known as a "drawing line." Such is the power of the pen. This, the exchange Ruy Lopez, as Fischer has shown, is not a drawing line but an invitation to an unbalanced endgame. As such it is ideal practice for the aspiring Candidate Master. He should familiarize himself with strategic play for both sides.

4... dxc6 5. 0-0 Qd6

This is a playable line but most modern players essay 5... f6 to hold on to the e-Pawn.

6. d4 exd 7. Qxd4

The Category I player rushes into the endgame, probably still under the spell of "the drawing line." What we have seen is that this position, with the two Bishops, can be a powerful point-scorer in the hands of a Candidate Master. For this reason, 7. Nxd4 tempting Black to develop White's game by exchanges would have been a better idea. We have already seen the Candidate Master using the two Bishops to win an endgame. Let us critique Black's endgame abilities in this game.

Diagram

7... Qxd4 8. Nxd4 Bd7

By castling long Black will occupy the open file and place his King on the side of the board where he has a Pawn more. The King can protect the c7 Pawn here, too.

9. Bf4 0-0-0 10. Nd2

The first sign that the player of the White pieces is not a Master. In Zuidema-Kosto 1967, White played 10. Nc3, a move that integrates his pieces better. White's problem in this opening is to find squares for his Knights. The ideal square is e4, after a properly timed e5.

10... Ne7

If Black can paralyze the White Kingside Pawns, prevent them from advancing, White will soon find he has no counter-chances against Black's 2B's. For this purpose Black plans to post his Knight on g6 where it eyes f4 and e5. Notice that if the Knight is driven from g6 by f5, the square e5 will be available to it. Notice that "mindless" development–development without a plan–by 10... Be7 will soon lead to a position where Black has few chances as a strong White center will keep Black's pieces out.

11. N2f3 Ng6 12. Bg3 c5

Black begins the by now familiar process of driving the White pieces from the center. This also opens up avenues for the white-squared Bishop. As White's pieces are driven back, Black's Bishops will grow stronger.

13. Nb3 Be7 14. Rfe1 h5!?

One goal of the holder of the two Bishops is to swap off his Knight for one of the White pieces. This brings the two Bishop ending closer. Black neatly accomplishes this by the threat of ... h4. For White to play h4 would drastically reduce his Bishop's scope and weaken his own Kingside Pawn majority. Therefore:

15. Ne5 Nxe5 16. Bxe5 f6 17. Bc3

Black has achieved his simplification. Now as a Candidate Master, what can be done to further increase Black's advantage? Analyse.

17... c4!?

Black had two lines of play. The attacking line based on 17... h4 may well succeed over-the-board, but Black does not have too many pieces to attack with. Instead he continues planning to drive the White Knight out of the center. After 18. Nd4, White's e5 is temporarily unappetizing as 18... Rhe8! (Notice the centralization on both sides) 19. e5?! fxe 20. Rxe5 Bf6! 21. Rxe8! (why not 21. Rxh5?) Bxe8! with a slight edge.

18. Nd2 b5 19. e5 Bc6!

Black plays with finesse–the two Bishops offer such opportunities. The Candidate Master needs only to be alert to such chances. He makes these chances happen by knowing the technique to "soften" up the opponent's position. The Category I player has been acquitting himself well, but even GM's have fallen to the power of the Two. What is Black's plan?

20. exf Bxf6 21. Bxf6 Rxd2! 22. Bxg7

White is not likely to survive the ending after 22. Bc3 Rxc2.

22... Rg8 23. Re7

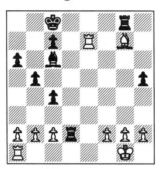

23... Rd7!

This insures the invasion of g2–White cannot defend by 24. R1e1 because of 24...Rxg7, winning.

**24. Rxd7 Kxd7 25. Rd1+ Kc8 26. Be5 Bxg2!
27. Rd2 Bh3+ 28. Kh1**

Black has broken through, but what now? Would even the gain of a Pawn be enough to win? Analyse.

28... c3!? 29. Bxc3 Bg2+ 30. Kg1 Bd5+ 31. Kf1 Bc4+ 32. Rd3

Based on the following continuation do you see why White could have had slight drawing chances without his 25th move? Omit 25. Rd1+ Kc8 and try 27. f3 Bxf3+ 28. Kf2 Be4 29. Rc1 Rg2+ 30. Ke3 Rxc2 31. Rxc2 Bxc2 Black will still have a chance to win, but he may be disappointed in the end.

But we observe in this position another peculiar happening when Candidate Master meets Category I player. Were you, too, taken in? Does c3 win? No. Analyse White's escape. Why does it happen that a player "believes" another player, believes him so much that he continues on a losing course? believes him so much he cannot find 29. bxc Bd5+ 30. Bg3! = A large part of this mental set comes from overrespecting one's opponent. The higher-rated does not usually suffer from this ailment; it generally afflicts the lesser-rated player. The Candidate Master must not worry too much about his opponent's rating. His job is to defeat his opponent. If he believes he can, he usually will; if he believes he is going to lose, he usually will. Rating points are a measure of an opponent's past performance, not how he will do in the particular game under consideration. Confidence grows with success, and success, at chess, is often closely related to the will to win, the sheer will to succeed.

But what has this missed line to do with the technique of 2B's vs. B+N? Only that the tactical chances favor the two Bishops. They are not always a forced win; they only give the holder the better chances when used correctly. The Candidate Master should learn to treat them with respect and assume he will find a win with them.

In our game, the Candidate Master found his "winning" line.

32... c5 33. Ke2 Rd8 34. Be5 Bxd3+ 35. cxd3

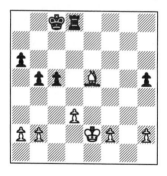

A new phase of the ending has developed: Black has a Rook against Bishop and Pawn. Can he win? What plan should he adopt?

35... Kd7

The King is to be brought to the center first. From its aggressive posture the Rook and King should find new inroads into White's position.

36. Ke3 Ke6 37. Ke4 Rg8 38. f4 Rg4 39. a3 Rh4 40. Kf3?!

White gives ground—after 40. Bb8 Rg4 41. Be5, Black has to find another plan. What would one winning attempt be?

40... Kf5 41. Kg3 Rg4+ 42. Kf3 Rg1 43. d4

White seeks to exchange Pawns, but this allows Black to tie him up.

43... cxd 44. Bxd4 Rf1+ 45. Bf2 Rd1 46. Ke2 Rb1 47. Bd4 Rh1

Notice that the CM does not hastily grab the f-Pawn. He knows the h-Pawn (freeing his own h-Pawn for queening) is more valuable.

48. Kf3 Rxh2 49. Kg3 Rd2 50. Be5 Rd3+ 51. Kh4 Rf3 52. Bg7 Rxf4+ 53. Kxh5 Rf1 White Resigns

Comment on the Candidate Master's endgame play. Could you do better?

42

THE FRENCH DEFENSE

1. e4 c5 2. c3

We have seen this opening a number of times already. The Candidate Master has several choices here. What are they? A well-prepared Candidate Master knows what line he will choose. Let us assume you are not so well-prepared and want to find a line that will restore equality of knowledge between the two combatants. Suggestions?

2... e6

This will soon transpose from Alapin's Sicilian to an Advance French–a line that may well not be in your opponent's repertoire. If it is, you are facing an opening expert with a Category I rating.

Is it cowardly to avoid White's 2. c3 challenge? This depends a lot on your concept of the chess battle. The fearless leap into 2... d5, the steady play 2... Nf6, the wary 2... e6. One chooses the opening line that fits one's temperament and knowledge.

3. d4 d5 4. e5 Nc6 5. Nf3 Qb6 6. Be2

White shows advanced knowledge (or memory) of this line, too. 6. Bd3 sets a cheapo–6... cxd 7. cxd Nxd4? 8. Nxd4 Qxd4 9. Bb5+ winning, but after 6... Bd7 White has to defend his d-Pawn or sacrifice it and perhaps the e-Pawn, too. This is an ambitious gambit, and the Black player must have great courage to gobble up both Pawns.

6... Bd7 7. 0-0 Rc8 8. b3?!

Alexander Alekhine once commented on copying the moves of the masters, "This short game once again shows the risks run by young players when blindly adopting certain innovations of the masters, without having carefully calculated all their consequences." After 8. dxc! Bxc5 9. b4 Bf8 10. Na3 with some Queenside initiative as in Antoshin-Bannik, USSR 1955.

But the Category I player's memory bank is out of data. His objective is not a bad one–the exchange of his dark-squared Bishop for Black's, but he will lose too much time doing it.

8... Be7 9. Ba3?! cxd 10. cxd Qa5 11. Bxe7 N8xe7 12. Qd2?

White's position was already weak, but this error drops the d-Pawn after which Black will have no problems. . . or will he?

12... Qxd2 13. N1xd2 Nf5

Diagram

After Black wins the d-Pawn, what should his plan be?

14. Rfd1 N5xd4 15. Nxd4 Nxd4 16. Bf1 Nb5

Black does not "rotely" castle. The King may well be needed in the center. Instead he probes at the weak White Queenside. The endgame will be won only if Black's pieces can harmoniously prepare the advance of the d-Pawn.

17. Rdc1 Ke7

The King is not only safe in the center, it supports an eventual ... f6 when it may be used to help advance the center Pawns. Black, of course, has no need for blindly exchanging by 17... Rxc1 18. Rxc1 when he is not ready to immediately contest the c-file.

18. b4 Nd4 19. Nb3

White's forces are greatly constricted by Black's d-Pawn which is why the one Pawn advantage is so strong in this position. White is trying hard to activate his pieces, but just can't do it. Black now may simplify further.

19... Nxb3 20. Rxc8

There was no good reason for White to initiate this exchange. If he is to resist at all, he will have to exchange off both Rooks. Why?

20... Rxc8 21. axb3 a6 22. f4

What should Black's general plan be at this stage?

22... Rc3

Black forces the White Rook to a passive position, limiting the strength of this piece. When the Rook becomes passive, Black can undertake some direct action to break into Black's position.

23. Ra3?! Bc6 24. Kf2 d4

Diagram

With the Rook in a passive state on a3, for the moment at least,

Black is playing with an extra Rook and Pawn. Black's main plan is to set his central majority rolling by 25... f6 ... fxe and ... Re3 winning the e-Pawn or 26. exf gxf and ... e5 with the Black Pawns moving strongly forward. White's next distracts Black from this plan, but his alternative plan wins easily enough.

25. Bc4!?

White's idea is 25... f6 26. Ra1 fxe 27. fxe Re3 28. Rd1 with some counterplay. Black plays steadily and erases White's Kingside—a sure road to victory without allowing White any counter chances. This is the steady play of a Candidate Master: no unnecessary risks in a winning endgame.

25... Rc2+ 26. Kf1 Bxg2+ 27. Ke1 Be4
28. b5 axb 29. Bxb5 Rxh2 30. Ra8

White's first active threat in the game. Black has a number of ways to win. What is the surest?

30... f6

If you selected 30... Bc6, recalculate. Move the pieces in your mind, not on your board. Do you see that 31. Bxc6 bxc6 32. Ra7+ Ke8 33. Ra8+ Kd7 34. Ra7+ will give White too much counter-play? By keeping the b-Pawn guarded, Black protects the second rank.

31. Re8+ Kf7 32. Rd8

Now the Candidate Master should see that 32... d3 33. Bxd3 Bxd3 34. Rxd3 Ke7 35. Rc3 Kd7 36. Rd3+ presents problems for

Black (who should still win, but the Candidate Master looks for solutions, not problems). What is a better plan?

32... fxe 33. fxe Kg6!

Black moves in on the cramping e-Pawn and soon the two passed Kingside Pawns will move inexorably forward. The Candidate Master should have no difficulties from this point.

34. Rxd4 Kf5 35. Rd7 g5 36. Rg7 g4 37. Be2 h5 38. Rh7 Kxe5

Black, of course, does not fear 39. Bxg4? Rh1+ 40. Kd2 hxg4.

39. Rh6 Bf5 40. Rh8 Kf4 41. Rc8 e5 42. Rc7 g3 43. Rxb7 h4 44. Rg7 h3 45. b4 Rh1+ White Resigns

43

THE KING'S INDIAN DEFENSE

1. d4 Nf6 2. Nf3 g6 3. g3 Bg7 4. Bg2 c5

Your opponent, who is almost a Candidate Master, is challenging you directly in the opening. You know you will have a battle before you. The question is how to conduct the campaign.

Some players note the time elapsed on their scoresheet. This notation only has value if the player studies the elapsed time on his scoresheet in order to learn to better balance his time in future games. Some suggestions for the Candidate Master may seem self-evident, but it is surprising how often the self-evident is violated even at the Candidate Master level. Such lessons are learned hard, if they are learned at all.

If a move is absolutely forced, the Candidate Master should not waste time calculating it. He can calculate the ramifications on his opponent's time. A logical corollary is that *given a choice of two moves, if the Candidate Master calculates that the first move is clearly losing and the other is vague and complex, the second move should be played without prolonged calculation.* Once again the Candidate Master can use his opponent's time to discover the secrets of the position.

5. c4

We have seen earlier that 5. d5 does not lead to much for White. The Candidate Master needs to store this information even if he doesn't play this line. Why? Someday the expert may decide to change his repertoire. Some experts like to experiment. Analysis of openings not in the Candidate Master's tournament play helps expand his knowledge of chess.

5... 0-0 6. Nc3 d5

We have arrived at a critical stage in the opening. This is the stage Botvinnik mentioned as the point to make plans for the middle game. Black spent 14 minutes deciding on 6... d5, and it may have caught the Candidate Master by surprise. Surprise moves by the opponent should be treated carefully. This is the critical moment that the advantage can be gained or lost, and as such, it is that moment that the most time should be invested.

Such an investment of time might reveal to the Candidate Master that the best way to strive for the advantage is 7. dxc!? Analyse this line.

7. cxd Nxd5 8. 0-0 cxd 9. Nxd4 Nc7

Black has spent a lot of time on this opening–34 minutes, leaving him with 56 minutes for the next 31 moves, but he has reached a position that is about equal. White has spent only 14 minutes, has lost his opening initiative, but has an extra 20 minutes. Who has come out of the position better? Now White goes in for a "long think"–15 minutes to find a move to strive for the advantage. But what if he had spent those fifteen minutes on move 7?

10. Be3 e5

Black is opening up the game while White is ahead in development. Can White take advantage of this? Analyse.

11. N4b5 Nxb5 12. Qxd8!?

The Candidate Master took twenty minutes to decide on this play leading into the endgame. His last six moves have taken 44 of his 90 minutes. This investment of time must produce results over-the-board or White will have to pay for it later. What plan does White have?

12... Rxd8 13. Nxb5 Nc6 14. Bxc6!?

This was White's idea, but he took another 14 minutes to calculate the coming endgame, leaving him 27 minutes for the remaining 26 moves. A rule of thumb for those who wish to avoid time pressure is not to fall behind the one minute-one move ratio. One way of saving time is, while your opponent's time is running, to calculate his best replies and your best responses to them. If he makes the expected response, you should make your move without too much delay. This anticipation can save valuable time.

14... bxc6 15. Nxa7 Bb7

What was White's response to 15... Bd7?

16. Rac1 f5 17. Rfd1 Rd5 18. b4 Bf8

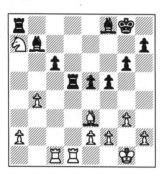

The Candidate Master has stolen a Pawn, but now he has 17 minutes left for 22 moves. He needs to simplify so that Black does not have the chance to complicate the position and distract White from his winning plan–which is?

19. Rxd5 cxd5 20. Rc7 d4 21. Rxb7 dxe3 22. a3 exf+ 23. Kxf2 e4

The simplification has occurred, the Candidate Master has matters well in hand. His handling of the clock has been adequate: he has 9 minutes left for 17 moves, a little touchy, but the position is not difficult. With a little care, White should have no difficulty in reaching time control.

The Category I player now violates a rule Fischer laid down–in lost positions you should not expend a lot of clock time trying to figure out a way to escape the lost game. This just gives your opponent more time (yours!) to calculate the win.

24. Nb5

Avoiding the last trap of 24. b5? when Black can play 24... Ra7, White eases in to win.

24... g5 25. Ra7 Rd8 26. Nc7 Bg7?!

This allows further simplification. Black might have tried 26... Bd6 ("hope" chess–27. Ra8? Bxc7!) but White should win easily enough with Ne6 and Nxg5.

27. Ne6 Bd4+ 28. Nxd4 Rxd4 29. b5 f4 30. gxf Rd5 31. b6 gxf 32. b7 e3+ 33. Kf3 Black Resigns

44

THE DUTCH DEFENSE

1. d4 e6 2. c4 f5

The Dutch Defense can be a strong weapon in the hands of a Candidate Master. Most players are not well-prepared against it and it presents some difficult problems to the lower-rated player.

3. Nf3 Nf6 4. Nc3 Bb4 5. a3

Although this gains the two Bishops for White, it leaves the Pawn weakness on c3 c4 d4 and a3. Aaron Nimzovich discussed how to best handle this Pawn complex in his work *My System*. The Candidate Master needs to be familiar with the exploitation of this Pawn weakness.

5... Bxc3+ 6. bxc3

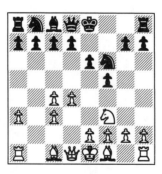

6... d6

First Black limits the Pawns mobility. For this reason 6... c5 is also playable.

7. g3

White's chances lay in opening up the position for his two Bishops. He also needs to watch his weakest Pawn (c4). For this reason e3, Bd3, 0-0, Nd2 and e4 with or without f3 will give him stronger play.

7... b6 8. Bg2 Bb7 9. 0-0 0-0

With his control of e4 and a good outpost for his "bad" Bishop, Black is at least equal in this position. White's Bishops lack immediate influence and his Pawns, though not yet under attack, are weak.

10. Re1 Qe8

The Queen is well posted here, covering two healthy diagonals. The Rook on e1 is not dangerous to the Queen until e4 is played. Analyse White's chances of successfully playing e4.

11. Nd2 Bxg2 12. Kxg2 N8d7

Good move or bad move? Comment.

13. e4

This is a critical point in the game. The Candidate Master has analysed this play. He knows if it is bad or good, and this knowledge is important for it will determine the course of the game. A Category I player playing Black, not sure of the position, might find 13... Qg6, but by analysis the Candidate Master will do what?

13... fxe 14. Nxe4 Nxe4 15. Rxe4 Nf6

Now we can answer the question asked on move 12. Black's plan was to prevent e4 by the developing 12... N8d7! The weakness on c4 now "miraculously" makes itself felt and Black gets a winning position.

16. Re1 Qc6+ 17. Kg1 Qxc4

The first phase of the opening is over. Black has won a Pawn and can expect to win the game. What further action should Black undertake after 18. Bd2?

18. Bd2 Rae8

This is a "natural" move, one that "looks" right. In general, moves that "look" right *are* good moves. Chess instinct tells us these are good moves. How does a Candidate Master develop this instinct? There are two ways–study and play. Study the games of the Masters, especially the modern ones and the World champions. Playing chess, tournament chess, postal chess, and 5-minute play is the other way to develop this instinct. Which is better? Probably play first and study a close second, but most important is the study of your own games to search for ways to improve.

19. Rb1 Qd3

The Candidate Master can see that White's forces are divided and not coordinating well with each other. For this reason he elects to go over to direct attack. Such board grasp is necessary for Candidate Master level decisions. Verify for yourself the non-integrated White pieces. How can White best orchestrate his pieces together. Is 20. Qe2 a try?

20. Re3

This is a typical "solution" of the Category I player–solving the short range problem but ignoring the long range. After 20. Qe2, White will probably lose also, but he can organize some play against e6 and the immediate danger of a Kingside attack is avoided.

Both moves 20. Re3 and Qe2 are about equal in value (they are losing moves in a losing position) but 20. Qe2 would offer Black more problems.

20... Qf5 21. f4

We can see that White's solution was no solution–his pieces remain discombobulated, his King's field is further weakened, and his Bishop becomes worse. Black needs to find the killing plan.

21... h5

Black sticks to his plan of Kingside attack, further tightening his grip on the white squares. White's position is grave. A Candidate Master who is a strong attacker should be looking for the way to KO his opponent quickly here. What is Black's attacking plan?

22. a4 c5

Evaluate this move. Evaluate 22... h4, the thematic continuation. Which one is preferable? Evaluate 22... Ne4. These would be the three main lines a Candidate Master needs to check in this position. In this position the Candidate Master believes he has to defend against Rb5 and counterplay by White. In his calculations, Black apparently could not fathom 22... h4 23. gxh Qxf4 24. Rxe6 but this was the right road. After 24... Qxh4 25. Rxe8 Rxe8, Black's attack is increased and he still has his Pawn plus.

When the Candidate Master cannot calculate, he should rely

on general principles. If he rejects 22... h4 because of its vagueness, he should elect another forward going line–both 22... Ne4 and 22... c5 answer that bill.

23. Rb2 Nd5 24. Rf3 cxd 25. cxd Qe4

The Candidate Master plays against White's weaknesses on the white squares. The Category I player has never found a way to balance his position.

26. Be1 Rc8

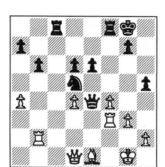

Black's plan of ... c5 bears fruit. The further open lines promise a further increase of his attack or transition into a winning ending.

27. Bf2 Nc3 28. Qd3 Qxd3 29. Rxd3 Nxa4

Black's theft of a second Pawn ends all effective resistance. Black need only be careful not to let White's Rook gain undue activity.

30. Ra2 Rc4 31. d5?!

White is understandably desperate, but this attempt to gain freedom for his Rook and Bishop only costs another Pawn.

31... exd 32. Rd4 Rc1+ 33. Kg2 b5 34. R2d2 Nc3 34. R4d3 a6 36. Bd4 Ne4 37. Ra2 R8c8!

The mark of the Candidate Master–he does not sit idly by and "let the position win itself," but enters into direct play to end the game. Analyse 38. Rxa6.

38. Kh3 R8c2 39. Rxa6 Rh1 40. Ra8+ Kh7 41. Bg1

Some players do not like to resign. The Candidate Master knows that checkmate is the best cure for such an attitude.

41... Rxg1 42. Rxd5 Rh1 43. Rxh5+ Kg6 44. Rxb5 R1xh2+ 45. Kg4 Nf6+ White Resigns

1. e4 c5 2. d4 cxd 3. c3

White is challenging you to a sharp battle. Should the Candidate Master decline by 3... d3 or accept by 3... dxc? or transpose by 3... Nf6? This is a question of temperament. White can probably maintain a slight edge against any of the three choices. The Candidate Master can thus choose the kind of warfare he likes best.

3... dxc 4. Nxc3 Nc6 5. Nf3 d6 6. Bc4 e6 7. 0-0 N8e8

This awkward-looking move is the blend of study and strategy. Black plays to strengthen the e5 square. By controlling e5, Black limits White's attacking chances. How does a Candidate Master learn such opening plans? By playing over master games, especially in variations you are likely to play, and noting ideas that you like. The Candidate Master keeps these ideas (not necessarily memorizing the exact order of moves) in mind. The chance to try out these ideas will arise if he plays often enough.

8. Qe2

The Category I player has learned a pattern in the Morra–Nc3 Nf3 0-0 Qe2 Rd1 Be3 or f4 or g5 and Rac1 with strong center pressure, but he fails to pose the most difficult problems to Black. By first playing 8. Bg5! he interferes with Black's positional treatment of e5 and keeps his chances alive. The reply, now or later, of ... h6 will weaken the g6 square when White will keep counterchances. This is how a Candidate Master approaches the position.

8... Ng6 9. Rd1 Be7

With e5 under control of the Black Knights, White has no chance for e5... Black is healthy in this position and has a Pawn plus.

10. Be3 0-0 11. a3

White is hard-pressed to find a means to develop attacking chances. Black is solid in the center and Kingside. The Category I player's gambit has failed. The Candidate Master now has to turn his central advantage to account. What is Black's plan?

11... a6

Black needs to prepare ...d5 by ...Qc7, ...Rd8, ...Bd7 (or ...b7) and subsequent opening up of the center. Before he can do that, he must equalize in development.

12. Rac1 Qc7 13. b4 Rd8

The Candidate Master is not careless– 13... b5? 14. Nxb5 axb5 15. Bxb5 Bd7 16. Bxc6 Bxc6 17. b5 would turn the game around, giving White a strong advantage. Black instead goes ahead with his game plan. White, striving for counterplay, will soon ruin his position against the reef of Black's solid, strong position.

14. b5 axb 15. Nxb5 Qa5

Usually in positions like this, the Queen finds safety at b8. The CM needs to carefully calculate Qa5 as his Queen does not have a lot of squares available.

16. Bd2 Qa4 17. Rc3

The Candidate Master will note the threat to his Queen, but unlike the lower-rated players, he does not seek to find a way to just save his Queen–he prepares a plan to use his Queen on a4. This is the Candidate Master at his best.

17... Bd7 18. Nc7 Rac8 19. Bb3 Nd4!

This was Black's plan–notice how much more effective it is to solve defensive problems using all one's pieces than to simply find a one-piece, one-move solution. This is the trademark of the Candidate Master.

20. Nxd4 Qxd4 21. Nb5 Bxb5 22. Qxb5 Rxc3 23. Qxb7

The game is over. Black merely has to make a few strong moves and the extra Rook will tell.

23... Rd3 24. Qb4 Qxb4 25. Bxb4 Rxb3 White Resigns

**1. e4 Nf6 2. e5 Nd5 3. d4 d6 4. c4 Nb6 5. exd cxd
6. Nc3 g6 7. Nf3 Bg4**

After 7... Bg7 8. h3 White has a small edge. Black is playing to wrest the central initiative from White. This is a dangerous undertaking when White has made no "wasted" moves. Such strategy is overplaying one's resources. It will generally work because the Candidate Master is a better chess player than his opponent; the Candidate Master must remember, though, that he was once a Category I player looking to upset an expert. The Candidate Master is a Candidate Master and not a Category I player because he plays sounder chess, not just more aggressive.

8. h3 Bxf3 9. Qxf3 Nc6 10. Be3 Bg7 11. 0-0-0 0-0

The Candidate Master should be happy with this position–he has achieved an unbalanced position where both sides have attacking chances. The winner will be the one who can devise the best use of his pieces. In other words, the winner will be the one who plays better. Analyse this position. What is Black's plan? What is White's?

12. c5

This is probably a surprise move and may unsettle a Candidate Master. Based on your advancing knowledge as a potential Candidate Master, what is Black's best treatment of this advance? Is this advance favorable or unfavorable to Black?

12... Nd7

Black waits to open up the game. This is, of course, quite logical as White has a slight edge in development. For White to play cxd only opens up the e-file for Black's pieces.

13. h4

This move should not come as a surprise–what is Black's defensive plan? What counterattack? What is your plan?

13... h6?!

This is not typical of a Candidate Master–this is pure defense in a situation that calls for something more. Black has two good lines that keep his position flexible–the Dragon-like defense 13... h5!? 14 g4 Nf6 or the better 13... Nf6. Both plans bring the passive Knight on d7 to the more active f6.

A gambling Candidate Master might try 13... Qa5 14. h5 dxc 15. hxg hxg 16. Qh3 Nf6 but it is unlikely he would be happy if the Category I player finds 17. Bh6!

Still, against a Category I player, even the gambling line would do better than pure passivity in such a double-edged position. Passivity has its place in balanced positions.

14. h5 g5 15. Ne4

Diagram

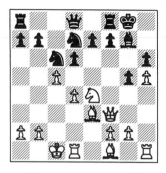

Black has periously compromised his Kingside. What plans can Black make to protect his King? Analyse.

15... f6?

A sad truth, but one that must be faced, is that all of us make bad plays from time to time. It is the obligation of the Candidate Master to make such bad plays less and less. Here, fear has pushed him into a horrible play. The threat of Nxg5 has driven our Candidate Master into a panic response. By keeping a cool head, Black should find 15... d5 to keep the center closed. Black enhances his survival chances and may yet find his counterattack come to life. What happens now is painful to contemplate.

16. Bc4+ Kh8 17. cxd e5

One of the most difficult lessons for the Candidate Master to learn is how to entrench, to defend a "totally" lost position. In this game he decides to throw the game into complications, but all the complications favor the attacking player who has a fairly clean line to win. Better was the more sanguine 17... exd. If an exchange goes, or a Pawn or two, Black may still find attacking chances–Category I players err too.

18. Qf5 exd 19. Bxd4 Nxd4 20. Rxd4 Rc8

Black's complications have produced nothing less than a beautifully centralized, Pawn plus, attacking position for his opponent. But he still has some breath, emphysemaic, but breath.

21. Kb1 Rxc4?!

This continues Black's suicidal play–the Candidate Master, in a lost position, should make his opponent find the win. Here, Black is still thinking defense only. After 21... Ne5 White may win, but he will have to find the way. The text gets rid of the attacking Bishop, but leaves White with an attacking Rook, plus the gravity of the exchange and a Pawn. There are times to sac the exchange. This is not one of them. Depression in a bad position can easily cloud judgement.

22. Rxc4 Re8 23. Rc7

Category I players, given the opportunity, know how to attack. Resignation would not be premature at this point.

23... Nb6 24. Rxg7! Kxg7 25. Qg6+ Kf8 26. Qxh6+

The Category I player has found an easy win. The Candidate Master would have been more efficient with 26. Nxf6 Qxd6 27. Nh7+! but this is little consolation to the Candidate Master.

26... Kf7 27. Re1 Rg8 28. Nxg5+ Rxg5 29. Re7+ Qxe7 30. dxe7 Kxe7 31. Qh7+ Ke6 32. Qxb7 Black Resigns

A brutal loss to the Category I player–a reminder that Category I players are always dangerous and must be treated with chessic respect. This is a game the Candidate Master should learn some hard lessons from.

Many Candidate Masters are willing–happy–to study their wins, to look for improvements in their play, but it is just such a catastrophe as this one that the Candidate Master can learn most from. It is not enough to pinpoint the flaws in the opening 7... Bg4 13... h6 a5... f6 etc., it is the thinking behind such decisions the Candidate Master must question and resolve to avoid in future contests.

This is a hard lesson to learn. Those who do learn, improve. Those who don't, make similar attitudinal mistakes again and again.

THE GRUNFELD DEFENSE

After facing some tough Category I players, we must not forget that as a Candidate Master you will also have to face some Category II (Class B) players. The Candidate Master needs to be efficient in defeating these lesser players. For a breather, then, you will face in games #47 and #48 a Category II opponent. As a Candidate Master follow along, plan, and study. You should expect to defeat your Class B opponent easily–not allowing him any dangerous counterplay–and score the point without too much difficulty.

1. d4 Nf6 2. c4 g6 3. Nc3 Bg7 4. Nf3 d5

The Candidate Master has to be sharp playing against a lower-rated opponent. Here, the Category II player has played a move that allows the CM to by-pass the sharp tactics of the extensively analysed Grunfeld exchange variation where the Knight will go to e2. With the Knight on f3, a more positional game is reached where the weaker player will have less chance to find strong moves.

5. cxd

The Class B player bites. An alternative is 5. Bf4 or 5. Qb3 but the White play tries to steer the game back into lines he "knows." He has fallen into the alert trap set by the Candidate Master.

5... Nxd5 6. e4 Nxc3 7. bxc3 0-0 8. Bb2

Diagram

The Candidate Master knows the theme of this position. What is Black's plan? Is the Bishop better posted on e3 or b2? Should Black try to play a complicated game or a simpler, thematic one? The position of the Knight on f3 and Bishop on b2 should help Black decide. Although both methods, tactical or positional, are likely to win, the positional method is both safer and more instructive (more likely to lead to further improvement) for the Candidate Master–but the Candidate Master also needs to be true to his style to some extent. It is this variety of choice that gives chess much of its attraction.

8... c5

Thematic: the attack on White's center will eventually produce a 2 to 1 Pawn majority on the Queenside for Black. This gives him a potential endgame edge. The middle game favors Black as White's center is shaky as the Knight on f3 which guards d4 may be challenged by ... Bg4. Of the two Bishops, Black's on g7 is better as it will be guarded after Black castles.

9. Bc4 cxd 10. cxd Qa5+ 11. Qd2 Qxd2+ 12. Nxd2?!

White is too interested in preserving castling rights, but 12. Kxd2 is right. The King is needed to protect the center. After 12. Kxd2 Nc6 13. h3 White is in the game and 12... Bg4 13. Rfd1 Nc6 14. Ke3 White is OK as ... Bh6+ Ke2 takes an attacker away from d4. Now White gets into trouble.

12... Nc6 13. Nf3 Bg4

Diagram

By simple, strong, and thematic play, Black has pushed White on to the defensive. Either 14. e5 leaving the d-Pawn weak or 14. Rd1 protecting d4 again doesn't seem appetizing so White decides to give up the d-Pawn in order to avoid becoming entirely passive, but he misses 14. Bb5 with some hope for counterplay.

14. Be2?!

How should the Candidate Master best win the Pawn?

14... Bxf3 15. Bxf3 Bxd4

White's plan was to play for opposite colored Bishops after 15... Nxd4 16. Bxd4 Bxd4. The endgame with a Pawn plus is easier with Knight against Bishop.

16. Rb1 Rac8! 17. 0-0 Bxb2 18. Rxb2 b6

Black has his Pawn plus. What are his next steps? Is this position won for Black?

19. Rd1

White will not be able to avoid the exchange of one set of Rooks, but he should try to avoid the swap of both pairs of Rooks. Why? The Candidate Master needs to grasp these ideas if he is to play the endgame well.

19... Rfd8 20. R2d2 Rxd2 21. Rxd2 Nb4

With the transparent threat of ... Nxa2. This allows further simplification.

22. a4 Rc1+ 23. Rd1 Rxd1+ 24. Bxd1

The Candidate Master has achieved his Rookless endgame. What plan should he have for the conduct of the endgame? What first? What next? Analyse.

24... e5

Black locks the e-Pawn to e4. By keeping the Pawn on a White square, he limits the scope of the Bishop. This also frees a path for the Black King, f8-e7-d6 etc., to the center. Then Black will create a passed Pawn on the Queenside by ... a6 and ... b5, by combining King, Knight, and Pawn. Black will force an exchange of Knight and Pawn for Bishop in such a way that his King will be left to invade and massacre White's Kingside Pawns. This is called the gravity of the extra Pawn.

25. Be2 Na2

Threatening to win immediately by 25... Nc3 and a Pawn goes.

26. Bd3 Nc3 27. Bc2 Ne2+

Black could speed the process up by 27... b5! but repositioning the Knight on d4 is not bad either.

28. Kf1 Nd4 29. Bd3 Kf8 30. Ke1 Ke7 31. Kd2 Kd6 32. Kc3 Kc5 33. h3 f6 34. Ba6 b5!

All according to plan. A Candidate Master must play the endgame logically.

35. axb Nxb5+ 36. Kd3 Nc7 37. Bc4 a5 38. h4 Kb4
39. g3 a4 40. f4 h6 41. fxe fxe 42. Bf7 a3 43. Ke3

White prefers to lose his Bishop rather than allow the winning procedure outlined above. After 43. Kc2 (gravity!) g5 44. hxg hxg 45. Ba2 Nb5 46. Bf7 Nd4+ 47. Kb1 (47 Kd3, Nb3!) Ne2 48. g4 Nc3+ 49. Ka1 Nxe4 and the Bishop cannot stop both Pawns.

43... Nb5 44. Kd2 Nd4 45. g4 Nb3+ 46. Kc2 a2
47. Kb2 a1(Q)+ White Resigns

The Candidate Master did not allow his weaker opponent any chances. It is this grasp of solid, sound play that will transform the Category I player to a Candidate Master.

1. e4 e6 2. d4 d5 3. e5

The advanced line in the French poses its own problems for the Class B player. It has the further advantage of being relatively unknown to most Category II players.

3... c5 4. c3 Nc6 5. Nf3 Qb6 6. Be2 N8e7

The Candidate Master may not have faced this move before. How can he best continue?

7. dxc Qc7 8. 0-0?!

The Candidate Master fails to solve the problem set before him. With 8. Nd4 he can keep the advantage as 8... Qxe5?! 9. 0-0 and b4 gives White the edge. Black loses after 8... Nxe5? 9. Nb5 Qxc5 10. Qd4! and Black has unanswerable problems. Why does our CM fail? Perhaps disrespect of his opposition. All opponents should be accorded a proper amount of respect. It should be the Candidate Master's attitude, however, that he will win, especially if he can get an unbalanced position.

8... N7g6 9. b4 Ncxe5 10. Nd4 Bd7 11. f4 Nc4!?

Black plays enterprising chess. Retreat by 17... Nc6 would give White less problems. Now, should White capture the Knight on c4 or play Na3? Analyse.

12. Bxc4

White cannot play 12. Na3, as the f-Pawn dies after 12... Nxa3 13. Bxa3 Nxf4 and White has no compensation after 14. N-B5!? Nxe2+ 15. Qxe2 Bxb5 16. Qxb5+ Qc6.

12... dxc4 13. a4 b6

The Candidate Master needs to be able to evaluate a position to determine if he stands better or worse. Evaluate this position. Once the Candidate Master has analysed the position, he can decide how to further conduct the game. Here the Candidate Master is in danger of letting the position slip away from him. He needs to "mix things up" to confuse the Category II player, to give Black chances to slip tactically. He must further be careful not to overextend his position lest the B player find the right defensive plays and emerge with an improved position.

14. Qf3 Rc8 15. cxb6 axb6 16. f5!?

Diagram

The Candidate Master, though in a slightly inferior position, knows how to pose problems. Now another Candidate Master might find 16... exf! 17. Nxf5 Bxf5 18. Qxf5 Bd6 19. Re1+ Be5 with advantage for Black, but few Category II players would find a line that gave up the two Bishops and pinned the remaining Bishop to his King. Now the game starts to swing to White's advantage.

16... Ne5?! 17. Qe4 Bd6 18. fxe6 Bxe6

To keep the two Bishops by 18... fxe6 leaves White with his

well-placed Knight on d4 and the Queen cut off from the Kingside, but White lacks the pieces to do anything meaningful. If Black were interested in playing for a win, this was his best choice.

19. Nxe6 fxe6 20. Na3

White's pieces begin to come out and the position shifts more and more to White's favor: this is the skill of the Candidate Master coming to the fore.

20... Qc6 21. Qe3

White elects *not* to play the favorable ending after 21. Qxc6+ Rxc6 22. Nb5 when Nd4 will be very bothersome to Black. This choice not to play the ending is partly justified by the exposed Black King and Black's handling of the last few moves. This is a matter of style. Most masters would choose the ending–against another master.

21... Rf8 22. Rxf8+ Kxf8 23. Bd2 Kg8 24. Nb5 Bb8 25. Nd4 Qd5 26. Qh3 Re8 27. Rf1

White has conducted his attack cleverly. His pieces are better placed, but only minimally, but he has recovered from his inferior opening. The next step is to find a winning plan. Note the Candidate Master has passed up 27. a5. He knows he can go back later with Ra1.

27... Ng6?!

The Category II player fails to appreciate that his position is at maximum strength. Black should wait with ... Bc7 and ... Bb8 until White disturbs the harmony of the position. This would give the Category II player defensive skills, however, that Class B players lack.

28. Qf3

Offering Black the chance of an endgame again. Should Black accept? Analyse.

28... Qd7?! 29. Qc6

White insists on his ending. Black must acquiesce. He would have thus saved a tempo or two by exchanging on move 28. The ending is only slightly in White's favor.

29... Qxc6 30. Nxc6 Bc7 31. Rd1!? Rf8

Latching on to the open file, but this is not an active contesting of the position. After 31... Ra8! White cannot continue with 32. Be3 Rxa4 33. Rd7 Be5 34. Nxe5 Nxe5 35. Re7 Ra1+ 36. Kf2 Ng4+ with good drawing chances. It is here in the ending that the Category II player plays to his rating.

32. Nd4 Rd8?

The blunder occurs because of time pressure. The Candidate Master cannot regret that the blunder "spoils the fight." Heartlessly (or heartened), he must now become the executioner. The Candidate Master must always be prepared for these shifts in the battle, just as he was in the opening.

33. Nxe6 Rd7 34. Nxc7 Rxc7 35. Be3

Black's one moment of inattention will cost him the game. Now the Candidate Master should put him away as efficiently as possible.

35... Ra7?

Helping out–time pressure has destroyed Black's game. The Candidate Master can learn, too, from his opponent's errors, in this case allowing himself to get into time pressure can ruin the fruits of the many hours' combat.

36. a5 Ne5 37. Bxb6 Rb7 38. Rd4 Re7 39. Re4 Rd7

Nothing matters.

40. Rxe5 Rd1+ 41. Kf2 Rd2+ 42. Kf3 Rd3+ 43. Re3 Black Resigns

49

THE NIMZOVICH DEFENSE

As a Candidate Master there will come the times when you will have to face a Master. You should look forward to such matches. A view of "I'm going to lose," should be avoided. Such a view usually guarantees a loss. Instead, you should look forward to such battles as an affirmation of your growing strength and an opportunity to cross swords and improve all the more. And if you should lose, you may have an opportunity to learn more about the game.

1. e4 Nc6

Already at move one the Master is setting problems: should the Candidate Master decline the opportunity to enter strange waters with 2. d4 or offer a chance to transpose into 2. Nf3? Since theory has it that 2. d4 is stronger than 2. Nf3, the Candidate Master should not shrink from trying his hand at White's first-move initiative.

2. d4 d5 3. e5

A Candidate Master who feels that his best suit is tactics might try the lines beginning with 3. exd. This would be the best play for the majority of Candidate Masters. In general, it is easier to beat a Master tactically than positionally. The 3. e5 line contains positional liabilities as well as assets that the Candidate Master may find hard to judge over the board.

3... Bf5 4. Nf3

The Candidate Master faces a difficult task here. With the Pawn position locked he must evolve a plan to encompass the rest of the opening and early middle game. By blocking his f-Pawn he may soon discover his center is unstable. Still 4. Nf3 should be playable in conjunction with Nh4 to exchange Knight for Bishop.

4... e6 5. Bd3

With his Pawns locked on dark squares, White should be reluctant to exchange his light-squared Bishop. The tempo gained after ... Bxd3; Qxd3 is not a real tempo as the Queen may not be well-placed on d3. A better location for the Bishop was on e2. Playing the Bishop to b5 is not good either as Bxc6+ bxc6 is not a threat as Black will soon be able to play ... c5. On e2, White can plan 0-0, c3, and when the d8-h4 diagonal is blocked, perhaps Nh4 to exchange the Bishop.

5... N8e7 6. c3

Worth a try was 6. Bg5

6... Qd7 7. 0-0 Bxd3 8. Qxd3 Nf5

The opening has ended. Evaluate the position.

9. Na3?!

The Candidate Master knows he has been outplayed to this point. Black's Bishop on f8 is better than White's on c1. Black has two possible Pawn breaks, ... c5 and ... f6 and White has none. His plan with Na3 is Nc2 and Ne3 to challenge the Knight on f5, but it allows a devastating retort by the Master. What is Black's best response to Na3? What would a better idea have been for White?

9... Bxa3!

Why is this move, exchanging Black's "good" Bishop so effective? The Candidate Master can and should learn from the Masters. Analyse the position after 10. bxa3. What will Black's plan be? What should White do to combat this plan? Answer to your own satisfaction why 9... Bxa3! is a good move before progressing.

10. bxa3 Na5

Now the obvious part of Black's plan comes to light, the light squares that is. The Candidate Master can particularly learn from the following plan. Is 11. Nd2 worth a try? Why not? What else can White do?

11. g4

Comment on this move. White is seeking active play very much like a wounded animal (a3 a2 c4) reacts by striking out in a rage. The Candidate Master has lost control of his game and emotions. This is a difficult lesson to learn (and one of those lessons that distinguishes Master from Expert). White has a bad game and will probably lose, but he should make life harder for the Master by 11. Rb1. The b-Pawn is untouchable, but White shouldn't weaken himself on both sides of the board. The Candidate Master should note that after ... Nc4 then Nd2 may lead to the exchange of the well-placed Knight at the slight expense of a nearly worthless Pawn on a3 for his bad Bishop or the Knight on d2. This would constitute resistance worthy of a Candidate Master.

11... Ne7 12. h3 h5

The Master is teaching the Candidate Master a lesson. It is a painful one, but from pain comes strength. Black does not leap into c4–that square will fall into Black's province when Nd2 is not available. Now White has a disagreeable choice to further bury his Bishop by g5, freeing the f5 square for the Black Knight or opening up the h-file. Which is preferable?

13. Nh2

After 13. g5, Black will castle long and play ... f6 when the Kingside will be ripped open. White elects a more defensive posture, but note how White's pieces are falling back, square by square.

13... hxg 14. hxg 0-0-0

Can White successfully exchange his bad Bishop for Black's Knight on e7? Analyse mentally 15. Bg5 Rdf8 16. Bxe7 Qxe7. Can White survive after 17. Qg3? Would this be worth a try in an OTB game? Notice that though this is White's best chance to survive, the Master has controlled both sides of the board. After White's maximum defensive effort, Black will switch to the Queenside and win a Pawn, or maybe two or three. The Master does not put all his pieces on one side of the board unless the decisive break will occur there.

15. Bf4 Nc4 16. Bg3 Rh3 17. Kg2 R8h8 18. f4

After this Black should have a forced win. The Candidate Master's attempt to find active play might work against lesser opposition, but will usually fail against the Master *with a positional advantage*. Such are the fates of Master versus expert. But such losses can be of value to the Candidate Master–if he studies both why he loses, and of equal importance, how his opponent wins.

18... f5

Sometimes these are called sledgehammer blows. Notice that 19. g5 will fail to 19...Qe8, ...Qg8 and ...Qh7 followed by ...Ne4 always linked with the possibility of ... Rxg3+. This is the result of the Master's strong play and the Candidate Master's early errors and active play.

19. exf gxf 20. f5

White is true to the end, always seeking activity, but now Black wins in clear-cut fashion.

20... exf 21. gxf Nd6

At last White's position collapses. Should the Candidate Master resign at this stage? No. He should learn from the execution, find out how the Master concludes a won game, and try to apply those lessons in his own games.

22. Rf3 N6xf5

Notice how the Master seeks simple solutions to difficult problems. The apparently more aggressive 22... N7xf5 allows 23. Bxd6! when White can hope to resist after 23... Nxd6 24. Nf7.

23. Nf1

Analyse 23. Rh1 and find a Black win.

23... Nxg3 24. Nxg3

What is Black's win after 24. Rxg3?

24... Rh2+ 25. Kg1 Qh3 26. Qf1

How does Black mate after 26. Rf2?

26... Rh1+! White Resigns

This was a particularly severe defeat for the Candidate Master, but there was much to learn from the game. Now set the pieces up and replay this game from the Master's point of view.

Once again you have to face a Master. Perhaps learning from the last game that the best way to fight a Master is to avoid a delicate positional struggle, you may resolve not to give ground, to fight the good fight. A positive attitude can be worth many rating points.

1. Nf3

The Candidate Master should play an opening he knows particularly well. If the Master should vary from the Candidate Master's book knowledge, the Candidate Master should assume (rightly or wrongly) that the Master's choice is inferior to the book line and play to refute it by his understanding of what his opponent's move "should" have been. This does not always work, of course, but it is a healthy approach.

1... d5 2. g3 c5 3. Bg2 Nc6 4. d4

If the Candidate Master is an expert with the Grunfeld Defense as Black, then this is a good choice as White. Black is unlikely to fall for the exchange variation as 4... cxd 5. Nxd4 e5 6. Nxc6 bxc6 7. c4 is much harder to meet a move down.

4... Nf6 5. 0-0 Bf5 6. c4

This is the staunch attitude described above. The CM is out to fight against the Master. Defensive play by 6. c3 is totally wrong. There is no reason why White, who has made only good moves so far, should assume a defensive attitude on move 6.

6... dxc

How can White continue? Analyse. Players familiar with the Catalan will recognize the pattern–7. Qa4 cxd 8. Nxd4! Qxd4 9. Bxc6+ Bd7 10. Rd1 and White keeps a slight edge.

7. Ne5!?

Although objectively 7. Qa4 is better, the text move has the advantage of challenging the Master directly. White's King is safe while Black's is still several moves from castling. The Master, confident in his own abilities, may enter into dubious complications. Black, of course, can't play 7... Nxe5.

7... Nxd4 8. Bxb7 Bc2 9. Qd2

What were the flaws behind 9. Qe1?

9... Be4!?

The Master offers an exchange in order to pursue his own attack. How should White proceed?

10. Bxe4!?

White is intent on aggression–a commendable attitude. Taking the exchange may be stylistic for some experts, but more than likely the Master will use the long diagonal and extra Pawn to defeat the mercenary style. Our Candidate Master has made up his mind that strong aggressive play is the best way to take a Master's measure. The weakness of Black's position is?

10... Nxe4 11. Qd1!

Operating with new threats, but how does White continue after 11... Qd5? Analyse.

11... Qd5 12. Nc3!?

Courage in the face of adversity–the logic of the position dictates the Knight on e5 must go. The Candidate Master in pursuit of his game plan must let the Knight die. As compensation Black's King will soon be under pressure from White's Rooks and Queen. Is this compensation enough? Perhaps not at the annotator's table or in correspondence play, but in the arena with the clock's inexorable ticking, it is the Master who will be under pressure. The Candidate Master needs only to find strong attacking moves: the Master must find how to prevent the loss. In such situations the Candidate Master has a real chance as long as he holds true to his plan.

12... Qxe5 13. Qa4+ Kd8 14. Bf4 Qf5

At first glance White has very little, a Knight and a Pawn down. The question is how safe is Black's King. The Candidate Master has banked on the King being vulnerable to attack. How would you evaluate this position?

15. Rad1 e5 16. Nxe4 Qxe4

Black has many opportunities to slip– 16... exf4?! 17. Qa5+, K-moves; 18. Rxd4 with an increased attack, but the Master is not likely to fall for this. But the clock ticks on and the Master has to analyse the complications. It is not easy to defend move after move in such a difficult position. How does White continue his attack now?

17. e3!

White has no need to think about defense. His goal is clear: continue the attack! The Master has no desire to remain forever defensive. He takes the opportunity to blunt White's attack, seeking some stability for his King. This is the technique of the Master but the Candidate Master remains with active pieces. The Candidate Master's gamble has, so far, succeeded.

17... Bd6!? 18. exd4 cxd4

White needs to find a way to continue his attack. His Bishop is attacked and Black is two Pawns plus. Analyse.

19. Qxc4!

This puts the Candidate Master solidly back into the game–he remains a Pawn down, but this is a far step from his investment of a piece a few moves ago.

The Master's problems still continue. Bad would be 19... exf4. Why? How does White continue after 19... Rc8? Is this Black's best defense (19... Rc8)?

19... f6

The Master in seeking to solidify his game rejects 19... exf4?

20. Rxd4 Qg6 21. R1d1 Ke7 22. Qe2+ wins outright. After the try 19... Rc8 20. Qxf7 exf4 21. Rfe1 Qc6 22. Qxg7 Re8 23. Qg5+ and White's attack continues with an unclear position. This in itself would be a reward for White's ambitious plan.

It might be noted that 19... Qb7! is more accurate here, but the text is also good.

20. Rfe1 Qb7 21. Rxd4!?

An important psychological moment–at the very moment Black seems to have completely consolidated his game, White strikes again, sacrificing an exchange to keep his attack alive. This is the Candidate Master at his best. Is the sacrifice sound?

21... exd4 22. Qxd4

White is operating on the premise that the threat is stronger than the execution, but 22. Bxd6 immediately is stronger: 22... Re8 23. Bc7+ Qxc7 24. Rxe8+ wins.

Now 22... Rc8 is met by 23. Be7+ Qxe7 24. Qxc8+ Kxc8 25. Rxe7 Rd8 26. Kf1 Rd7 27. Rxd7! and White wins the King and Pawn ending. Verify this. 22... Kxd7 23. Ke2 Kd6 29. b4! Kd5 30. Kd3 f6 31. a4 f5 32. a5 a6 33. f4 winning.

22... Qb6?

After finding 21 good moves in a row, the Master slips, a .955 batting average, but sometimes that percentage is not enough. An inspired Candidate Master can, on the right day, score against *anyone*. Such results are the summation of all the skills and tricks accumulated by the Candidate Master in the course of learning. The Candidate Master who aspires to be a Master might be interested in a further book in this series *How To Become a Master*, but that is for the future. For now White must plan on how to put his opponent away.

23. Qd5 Rc8 24. Bxd6 Qc6 25. Qd4 Qd7 26. Be7+ Kc7
27. Qxa7+ Kc6 28. Rc1+ Black Resigns

So we see, it can be done. All that remains for you, the Candidate Master, is to go out and do it. Desire is half the battle; the other half is study, practice, learning, and skill.

OPENING INDEX
(by page number)

Colophon

This book was set in Cardinal. Typography by *typefaces, inc.*, 331 Union Arcade Building, Davenport, Iowa 52801. Cover Design by Rick Reed.

Typesetting by Pat Pimlott and Bob Long.

The · THINKERS' PRESS · List

Since 1967 we have been publishing for the chess enthusiast. Our publications are professionally manufactured.

We are known for original material whether it is an openings book or a research document. Our shipping department handles all orders within 24 hours.

For ☎ orders dial (319) 323-7117 anytime.

Our ISBN is listed with each of our publications in the upper left corner. Our stock number is located before the price. Please use our catalog number when ordering.

❖ BACKLIST ❖

0-938650-08-4
Predicament in 2-Dimensions: *Ariel Mengarini, 3rd printing*
How to think about chess in an organized manner. Witty, intellectual, and thought provoking. Includes 3 dozen master level games (annotated).
105 + vi pp., alg. not. B1.1828.ME1.000 **$8.50**

0-938650-10-6
Correspondence Chess: *Hanon Russell*
The best overall accounting of postal chess (and other forms) you will find in English. Includes many great games, history, tables, and miscellaneous information to get you started into this fascinating area.
186 + iv pp., alg. not. G1.2710.RU1.000 **$10.95**

0-938650-13-0
Chess On Stamps: *Bob Long, reprinted from "Chess Life", 1974*
Features stamps (many photos) and writeups about their connection with the chess world (Olympiads, Famous Players, World Championships, etc.). Many beautiful miniature works of art.
7 pp. F1.3100.RL1 **$2.00**

0-938650-14-9
Romanishin Variation (4g3) of the Nimzo-Indian Defense: *Barry Spiro*
A new method for handling this tough defense from the White side. A major plus is the research involving transpositional lines from other openings.
30 pp., alg. not. O1.0534.SP1.000 **$4.50**

0-938650-15-7
Persona Non Grata: *Viktor Kortchnoi & Lenny Cavallaro*
The tribulations caused by defecting, from the Soviet Union, in his bid for the World's Champion title.
Thorough annotations to 7 of the games from the 1978 match, 3 by Kortchnoi, and 2 each by Alburt and Shamkovich. Other games given without notes.
"A work of great importance...must reading"—George T. Stanton, CIA (retired).
147 + viii pp., alg. not. . . . . paper B1.1770.KC1.000 **$8.95**
. . . . hardcover B1.1770.KC1.010 **$19.95**

0-938650-17-3
The Meran and Rubinstein's Anti-Meran: *T.M. Tucker*
An historical study coupled with extensively annotated games. Rubinstein's greatness is exemplified by seemingly simple refutations to systems that had been around for awhile.
63 + iii pp., fig. alg. O1.0850.TU1.002 **$6.95**

0-938650-18-1
Endgame Artillery: *Alex Angos*

A master treatise about high powered endings. Rave reviews. Queen and Rook artillery.

109 + i pp., alg. not. E1.1260.AN1.000 **$10.95**

0-938650-21-1
My Chess Adventures: *C.W. Warburton*

A master of the Lopez and one of Great Britain's top correspondence players recounts his exciting games and career. The excoriating pen and the strong hand provide the reader with hours of pleasure from difficult subjects to miniature postal games. 32 chapters.

201 + ix pp. B1.2175.WA1.001 **$14.95**

0-938650-25-4
The Anti-Indian: *Allan Savage*

A complete accounting of Trompowski's Attack by a FIDE master. A method for avoiding a plethora of fianchettoed Bishops. Pawn formations and many new games are included.

58 + iii pp., alg. not. O1.0930.SA1.000 **$9.00**

0-938650-27-0
The Sicilian Wing Gambit: *John Hurt*

An optimistic approach to the dreaded Sicilian Defense by one of its staunchest advocates! Hundreds of new games and notes along the lines of *MCO*.

49 + iv. pp, alg. not. O1.0838.HU1.900 **$7.00**

0-938650-30-0
Grandmaster Fearless: *ed. by Bob Long*

Accounts of Kortchnoi's four wins of the powerful U.S.S.R. chess championship, a feat that hasn't been surpassed! Should be read with *Persona Non Grata*. Includes statistics of his play against all the living world champions.

16 pp., alg. not. B1.1770.LO1.000 **$2.00**

0-938650-31-9
Viktors Pupols, American Master: *Larry Parr (ed. of "Chess Life")*

Enter the whacky world of one of America's most eccentric and brilliant chess masters. Fantastic exploits of a legend in Northwest chess. Explosive games and temperament. Praised by many and excerpted in *Chess Life* magazine.

79 + x pp., alg. not. B1.1935.PA1.000 **$6.50**

0-938650-32-7
The King's Gambit As White: *Robert Raingruber, Lou Maser & Larry Christiansen*

The book for aficionados of the KG. The recommended variation is 5 Ne5. Also included are the declined variations and the Falkbeer Countergambit. Organized like a textbook for study. Extremely popular.

173 + iii pp., alg. not. O1.0410.CMR.000 **$14.95**

0-938650-34-3
Salo Flohr's Best Games of Chess: *Gregory Donges*

At last, a book about the grandmaster who won the Hastings tournament more times than anyone else, one of the strongest players in the 30's.

This book is full of sparkling games and combinations.

102 + iv pp., alg. not. B1.1615.DO1.000 **$9.00**

✿ OTHER TITLES WE DISTRIBUTE ✿

Lacking the Master Touch: *Wolfgang Heidenfeld*
A masterful book on wending your way through master and grandmaster opposition by having confidence in yourself and your own material. Heidenfeld was one of chess' best writers.
115 pp. . . . . .hardcover B1.1675.HE1.011 **$9.95**

Secrets of a Grandpatzer: *Kenneth Colby*
The lessons of a lifetime distilled in one book. Many have told me they had to read 15 different books to find out the hardway what is printed in this ONE book.
Subtitled, *How to Beat Most People and Computers at Chess.*
140 pp., fig. alg. not. . . . . .hardbound M1.1190.CO1.012 **$20.00**

LASKER & HIS CONTEMPORARIES

In 1978 we began publishing a series about Emanuel Lasker and the Golden Age of chess. Edited by Bob Long, contributors have included Wolfgang Heidenfeld, C.J.S. Purdy, GM Larry Evans, Dr. Nathan Divinsky, Dale Brandreth, and of course Lasker!

Translations, theories, photos, new articles, and some incredible game annotations cover Lasker and the other giants of chess. The fifth issue will cover Lasker's mathematical career, Steinitz, and much more.

An oasis in a Sahara of chess literature. All are 8½x11 format.

0-938650-22-X
Issue One: Capablanca-Lasker negotiations, Lasker's profundity, the Earliest Recorded Lasker Game, Annotated Games, and the Ten Best Controversy.
36 pp., ...B1.1790.LO1.000 **$7.00**

0-938650-23-8
Issue Two: The Great Steinitz Hoax, Karl Schlechter, 1903 Lasker-Chigorin, Lasker the Mathematician and the 1910 Lectures.
40 pp. B1.1790.L02.000 **$7.00**

0-938650-24-6
Issue Three: Lasker vs. the Devil, New York 1893, Frank Marshall, Chess & Strategy, Lasker's Forgotten Games and Lasker in the U.S.S.R.
48 pp. B1.1790.L03.000 **$8.00**

0-938650-26-2
Issue Four: Doomsday Encounter, Khrulev on Lasker, Cambridge Springs, Marshall and Lasker, 1894 Match, Lasker's Visit to Spain, Chess Nerves and the Annotated Lasker.
56 pp. B1.1790.L04.000 **$10.00**

The Lasker Poster: A beautiful, full size two-color rendering of the artwork designed by Bob O'Hare for *Lasker & His Contemporaries.* Orange-brown & black. Great for framing. Sent in mailing tube (shipping is extra). Minimum order is 5.
. . . .**$9.95**

Thinkers' Press
1026 Arlington Court
Davenport, Iowa 52803 U.S.A.
☎ 319 323-7117

Answer Guide to
How to Become a Candidate Master

We had many requests, from buyers of the first edition of *How to Become a Candidate Master,* for an answer guide to the questions posed inside of this book.

Now such a booklet is available!

Besides that, the ratings of the 50 players are given as well as a complete rundown on typographical errors and corrected diagrams.

Mr. Dunne has graciously provided us with a brief biographical sketch and will begin also conducting a column on "chess miniatures" for *Chess Life* magazine starting with the December 1986 issue. He has also begun work on a novel, nothing connected with chess. His newest work is *How to Become a Class A Player* in which the same type of format is used. This book will also approximate HTBACM in size.

Send **$3.95** today for your postpaid copy

Thinkers' Press
1026 Arlington Court
Davenport, Iowa 52803

MasterCard and Visa welcomed